MO[...]
FOO[...]
IS RUBBISH

An A–Z of all that is wrong with
'the beautiful game'

MODERN FOOTBALL IS RUBBISH

An A–Z of all that is wrong with 'the beautiful game'

Nick Davidson
& Shaun Hunt

SPORTS
BOOKS

Published in Great Britain by
SportsBooks Limited
PO Box 422
Cheltenham
GL50 2YN
Tel: 01242 256755
email: info@sportsbooks.ltd.uk
www.sportsbooks.ltd.uk

Cover design by Nick Davidson

A catalogue record for this book is available from
the British Library.

ISBN 978 1899807 71 0

Printed by Creative Print and Design, Wales.

Acknowledgements

Nick Davidson

For Kathryn, Bessy & Charlotte who I love with all my heart.

Dad, my companion at football for all these years; Mum for all your love and support; Nicky Robinson, Steve Lowe, Martin Godleman & Frazer Payne for their advice; The Chunk for laughing in all the right places; Mike for masterminding a sales surge from his island lair; Rach for reminding me about the vagaries of stud pressure (The New Inn, 1992, right?); Welshman for modelling t-shirts in Hamburg; Helen; 'Uncle' Kev; Lee & everyone at Driftgate; Shaun whose contributions to this book are the funny ones.

Shaun Hunt

Helen, for loving me and tolerating my obsession with football. Jay and Laura, my beautiful children.

For all your support: Mum and John, Simon and Katie, David and Louise, Brian and Rita, Jayne and Des, Scott and Todd; Kathryn, Bessy and Charlotte for your friendship and support; all Spleens, wherever you are; everyone at Port Isaac FC, Noel Clarke and everyone at Cadbury Athletic FC; "King" Kenny Dalglish and Liverpool Football Club for inspiration; Nick Davidson, best mate, whose genius I am riding on the coat tails of.

Africa Cup of Nations

The Africa Cup of Nations is our favourite international football tournament. We like it because it comes round so quickly. It's biennial, unlike its European counterpart which is only played every four years.

We also like the fact it is usually played in January and February. Those are pretty dismal months for football – eight weeks of frozen pitches and hamstring injuries – a time when anyone with any sense seeks refuge inside John Motson's sheepskin coat and awaits the first signs of spring. But every other year, our lives are brightened by a festival of football beamed via satellite from a far-flung corner of Africa.

Thanks to the Cup of Nations, the end of January and the beginning of February becomes a time of staying up late (usually on a school night) to catch Garth Crooks, Efan Ekoku and Gavin Peacock on the BBC2 graveyard slot.

So, hats off to the Beeb for screening the tournament and adding some excitement to a depressing time of year. And thankfully, the rest of the football media is so Eurocentric that it is quite possible to get through the day without finding out the results. This means we can sit back and enjoy the highlights – just like we used to do in the good old days.

Unfortunately, not everyone shares our enthusiasm for a mid-season international tournament. In fact, the mere mention of the Africa Cup of Nations is enough to send some club managers into a fit of apoplexy.

You see, most managers are none too happy when their star names jet off to Africa for a month, slap-bang in the middle of the domestic season. Funny that, because unless they are really signing a player on the evidence of thirty seconds' worth of YouTube footage they should have realised their new signings were, well, African.

Next come the calls for Africa to fall in line with the rest of the international calendar by moving the tournament to the summer months. These demands to reschedule smack of neo-Colonialism. Why don't we just get a ruler and a pen and draw some arbitrary borders all over the continent? Oh yeah, our forefathers did that already.

Managers moaning is one thing but, prior to the 2008 tournament in Ghana, Sepp Blatter dispatched the FIFA gunboat to fire a few warning shots across the bows of the CAF, insisting that the tournament must be held in June or July by 2016. When Sepp looks out of his office window in June or July, the weather is probably quite pleasant. However, it wouldn't really be the Africa Cup of Nations if it were played in Zurich, would it Sepp? Africa is vast and some parts of the continent would never get to host the tournament if it were moved to June or July – a time when parts of Africa are in the grip of the infamous 'long-rains' while other areas swelter in unbearable heat. Not exactly ideal conditions for a major international tournament, eh?

Then there's the history. People also forget that the competition has been held during the European football season for the majority of its fifty-year lifespan. It is only since the arrival of large numbers of talented African players in the big European leagues that the tournament's timing has become an issue.

In fact, the Africa Cup of Nations is older than its European equivalent. It was first played in 1957, a full three years before the first European Nations Cup. Why should Africa tinker with tradition just to placate a few disgruntled club managers?

Of course, the ultimate irony is that the Cup of Nations usually produces a star player or two, sparking a transfer frenzy among the very same managers who have spent all month whingeing about the competition. In fact, a BBC survey conducted during the 2008 tournament revealed fifteen of the twenty clubs in the English Premier League had sent scouts to Ghana. If clubs are happy to plunder the continent for talent, it is about time they showed the continent some respect.

So, let Africa enjoy her tournament. Let us enjoy Africa's tournament and let the managers and bureaucrats moan as much as they like.

At home with the stars

Imagine a world before *Hello!* magazine. It's not easy is it?

These celebrity mags have long since cornered the market on photographing showbiz weddings or capturing the stars on film in luxury island hideaways. But life for a professional footballer hasn't always been about securing exclusive image rights for star-studded weddings. Cast your mind back thirty years, and your average player was more than happy to let the *Shoot!* photographer into his house to take a few snaps for a feature ambitiously titled 'At home with the stars'.

What really struck us flicking through old copies of *Shoot!* is that these guys were just like you and me. They were seemingly content with a modest bungalow or a semi in the suburbs. Occasionally, a shaggy-permed midfielder would've invested his signing-on fee in a cottage in the country, but that was as extravagant as it got. These were regular blokes who owned nothing more ostentatious than a new hi-fi or a colour telly.

The photos that the *Shoot!* snapper took were even more revealing. These professional sportsmen clearly enjoyed lounging about at home wearing their international caps and weren't ashamed of being photographed mowing the lawn with their shirts off. True, the feature had a certain *Life on Mars* quality about it – wives and girlfriends were usually photographed bringing the star his tea, or vacuuming the lounge whilst our hero remained firmly ensconced in his armchair. And our hero would often be captured on film fingering the new Linda Ronstadt LP with a caption that read something like 'Brian loves her voice – *and her looks!*'

But these were simpler times. Times when a top-flight footballer might still have lived round the corner, rather than miles away in an opulent mansion on some gated development, replete with a 6ft plasma TV in the khazi.

Authority

We cannot remember many referees from the 1970s and '80s. In fact, we think there were only two: Clive 'The Book' Thomas and Jack Taylor.

We might not recall their names but we remember one thing – they had authority. Players respected them.

There was no doubting who was in charge. You got the impression that Clive or Jack would've been happy to cuff any dissenting players around the back of the head, if only the rules had allowed it. Certainly anyone brave enough to rule out Zico's last-minute 'winner' against Sweden at the 1978 World Cup had to have balls.

We all know loads of refs these days. We know them because they are crap. And we know them because they are always on our TV screens. Gone are the respectable school-masters, who saw refereeing as a natural extension of their day job – upholding the morals and discipline of the nation. Instead, we are left with a bunch of egotistical wanabees, self-obsessed maniacs who probably tried and failed to get into the *Big Brother* house. They crave attention. They shouldn't be wasting time on media training courses to hone their post-match interview technique. Instead, lock them in a room with a class full of cocky teenagers and see how they cope.

In recent years only Pierluigi Collina has come close to earning the respect of players. Why? Well, because he could do that scary thing with his eyes but also because he had buckets of authority.

Of course, it doesn't help that they wear yellow and pink shirts these days.

Black is for referees, green is for goalkeepers. Simple.

Autobiographies

Walk into any bookshop in the run-up to Christmas and you'll be confronted by a wall of 'celebrity' autobiographies. Is there a better yardstick for how shallow society has become? Shouldn't we be encouraging people to read Shakespeare, Keats or Dan Brown?

Once you've discarded the celebrity chefs, the ex-*Big Brother* housemates and Kerry Katona, you'll be left with an unfeasibly large number of books by footballers.

There used to be a time when players waited until the end of their sodding careers before sitting down with Harry Harris for a pint and a chat. These days the average age for a Premiership player's autobiography is twenty-four*.

T-w-e-n-t-y e-f-f-i-n-g f-o-u-r-! That's not a life story. It's a glorified school report.

All footballers' books follow the same tired format. Here's the template that was handed to us, in a gloomy Fleet Street pub, in exchange for a large Scotch. It requires the minimum of fleshing out:

1. Played football in the street (a lot).
2. Went to school. Didn't like school much. Captained school team. Scored 376 goals in a single season.
3. Was expelled from school.
4. Signed YTS forms for local club.
5. Broke into the first team.
6. Broke into England squad.
7. Got a celebrity girlfriend.
8. Got caught 'playing away'.
9. Missed a penalty and/or sent off in crucial World Cup game.
10. Got a six-figure book deal.

Even the titles are interchangeable. If you've got an ordinary sounding name it will be a simple: *Ryan Giggs – My Story*.

If you've been lucky enough to have a nickname it will be something flamboyant like: *Robbo – My Story*. And if you've been to hell and back, hitting all the highs and the lows that professional football can offer you, your book will probably be called: *Gazza – My Story*.

Things got really out of hand after England's appalling performance at the 2006 World Cup. Days after England slunk out of Germany following another penalty shoot-out failure, lame autobiographies started to fill the shelves of WH Smith's. Steven Gerrard, Ashley Cole, Wayne Rooney and Frank Lampard all cashed in on failure by releasing books that devoted chapters to England's World Cup disaster.

But as we cried into our beer and got our knickers in a twist over that little winker, Cristiano Ronaldo, the suits from Harper Collins must have been dancing around the boardroom with joy. Why? In March 2006, Wayne Rooney signed the biggest sports book deal in publishing history – a five-book deal reportedly worth a staggering five million pounds. Rooney's stamp on Ricardo Carvalho might have cost us a place in the World Cup semi-finals but it would've done wonders for sales of, yes, you've guessed it: *Wayne Rooney – My Story So Far*.

There is so much to loathe about footballers' autobiographies. But what really gets our goat is not the uninspired titles or the dodgy prose – it's the awful covers. If we have to look at one more moody photograph of a perfectly groomed footballer posing in his civvies, we will be forced to drive a truck through the window of Waterstone's. Look, publishers, it's not rocket science – we already subscribe to the *Next Directory*. If we are buying a book about a footballer we want to see him on the cover lifting a trophy or celebrating a goal, not looking like an outcast from a mailorder catalogue.

In their football gear it is almost possible to rationalise the money and the adoration heaped upon them. Shorn of their kit, they just look like ordinary blokes, and that is really depressing.

* Possibly. We've not actually checked.

Benny or Ziggy

Grange Hill revolutionised children's programming in the late 1970s. Gritty storylines featuring kids giving teachers plenty of lip made the show essential tea-time viewing. Everyone had their favourite characters: Trisha Yates, Scruffy McGuffy, Roland, Gonch, Danny Kendall or even Mr Bronson. Tucker Jenkins, the rebel with a heart, even managed his own spin-off series on BBC2, *Tucker's Luck*, where he struggled to cope with life in the real world, armed only with a CSE in metalwork.

For football-obsessed kids like us, who regarded school as a kickabout with your mates interrupted by lessons, *Grange Hill* taunted us with the occasional subplot involving the beautiful game.

In the early series, one of Tucker's mates, Benny Green, was frequently shown carrying a football – occasionally he even got to kick it. Benny was good enough to be selected for the district team, which for schoolboys at the time was the height of ambition. Unfortunately for Benny, the match clashed with a school fixture, and the PE teacher, Mr Baxter (he of the tracksuit and the whiskers) was determined to make him play for the school.

However, in a trademark TV dilemma, Benny stood up for himself and went to play for the district. Baxter could only admire Benny's resolve. Sadly, Benny's football prowess was left entirely to the imagination. Either the budgets wouldn't stretch to filming a proper match, or the real-life Benny was shit at football. We will never know. Benny drifted out of *Grange Hill* and didn't even reappear in *Tucker's Luck*.

Football died a death as Zammo's drug-taking took centre stage. But then, almost unnoticed, a new character was ushered in, just in time to star in the legendary 'Just Say No' video.

With Liverpool and Everton ruling the roost in the '80s, it was no surprise to see the next *Grange Hill* football sensation was scouse. Ziggy Greaves arrived at the school and quickly showed off his skills. Happy-go-lucky and always up for a prank, Ziggy's football storylines were not relegated to a sideshow like Benny's. In one episode, the school's battle for the Cup included actual footage of Zig playing footy. As with most teenagers, other interests distracted Ziggy in his later years; while Benny faded away, Ziggy moved to back to Liverpool after finishing his GCSEs. But not before copping off with the lovely Georgina in his final episode. Georgina or football? Yeah, we'd have chosen Georgina too.

So who was the better player, Benny or Ziggy? We'll never know for sure, but whether it was the single-minded, mysterious Benny, or the easy-going, warm-hearted Ziggy, we all identified with their passion for football.

Poor Benny and Zig, their love of the game came twenty years too early. Had they been around these days, they'd have had lucrative careers on the pro-celebrity football circuit. Instead, they've had to seek alternative forms of employment.

Big four, the

They're big, there are four of them and they won't let anyone else play.

Billy's Boots

F**k Jamie and his Magic Torch, we dreamed of magic boots. Imagine becoming the best player in your school – overnight? For one lucky kid this dream came true. He lived with his Gran, he discovered an old pair of boots in the loft and – hey presto – he was transformed into a football genius. Unfortunately, he wasn't real.

Billy Dane was something of a comic-strip journeyman. He first appeared in *Scorcher* in 1970; he then moved to *Tiger* where he stayed for several years before the comic merged with *Eagle*. Finally, a high-profile transfer had Billy seeing out his days at *Roy of the Rovers*.

Billy's boots had belonged to a former professional striker, Dead Shot Keen. They were magic boots: with them Billy was unstoppable; without them he was next to useless. Considering these boots were so bloody brilliant, he didn't take particularly good care of them. In fact, he seemed to lose them on a weekly basis. They would regularly fall in the river and have to be fished out miles downstream. Or the tough kids at school would steal them from his bag. This would usually happen just before kick-off in a very important cup match. The boots weren't even safe at home. His Gran was always minutes away from throwing them in the bin. When storylines were in short supply, he even managed to get hold of some magic cricket boots – what are the chances of that?

For a number of reasons – none of them to do with magic – Billy and his boots wouldn't survive for five minutes in today's culture.

Billy wore a pair of battered, old, second-hand boots. Old? Used? These days, kids rarely have anything 'used' unless it's off eBay and their parents foist it upon them. Spend an afternoon down the park watching youth football and we defy you to spot a pair of boots not from this season's range. Most kids have two pairs of boots, for use on soft and firm ground. Add in a pair of astro-trainers, and modern kids are a walking branch of JJB Sports.

There are certainly no hand-me-downs on offer. The fact that modern boots are so flimsy that they rarely last more than one season is a separate issue but we're pretty certain that Billy wouldn't even bother to turn up for practice today if he had to wear those tatty old boots. The other kids would just take the piss.

Also, Billy was an average player when he wasn't wearing the boots, yet he was rarely dropped. While it is true that 'form is temporary, class is permanent', have a bad game in today's instant culture and you are written off. Billy would be out of the team. What would he do with his magic boots then? Flog them on eBay?

Billy was a product of his time. Kids do not read stories about football. Why do they need to in the age of 24-hour reporting and dedicated football channels on the telly? There is no room for fantasy in modern football – which is even more reason to keep searching for it.

Books about football finance

This book is living proof you can get any old tosh published – as long as it is about football.

At the end of the '90s publishing houses were falling over themselves to release books about the financial crisis in the modern game. Any goon who'd spent three years at the LSE and ninety minutes at White Hart Lane was writing a book about football finance. Some of them were probably quite good. We wouldn't know, we've not read them.

Titles like *The Economics of Football* or *The People's Game: Football, Finance and Society* were enough to put us off, although *Broken Dreams: Vanity, Greed and the Souring of British Football* sounds right up our street.

We're sure all these books are well-intentioned and meticulously researched but, let's face it, you don't have to be John Maynard Keynes to work out what's wrong with modern football. It's simple – there's too much money in the game.

Television pays too much money for broadcasting rights. Clubs pay too much money for players. And, as a result of all this nonsense, fans are charged far too much money to watch a game. As long as this inflationary spiral continues, football is doomed. There's no sign of the bubble bursting. TV deals get more preposterous, the first £100 million player is, surely, only a couple of transfer windows away and tycoons, oligarchs and heads of state are still queuing up to buy into the Premier League. Football has lost its sense of worth. We wouldn't be surprised to switch on the latest instalment of *Footballers' Cribs* and find that one of these overpaid dandies has wallpapered his entire mock-Tudor bachelor pad with £50 notes.

The parallel with the German hyper-inflation of the 1920s is uncanny. And we all know how that ended, don't we?

We are guessing that the multitude of books on football finance draw similar conclusions. We can only guess because, like we said, we've not read any of them.

Championing the wonder-kids

Manchester United's signing of a nine-year-old 'YouTube wonder-kid' caused a right old furore in the media. Some were hailing the lad as the new Wayne Rooney, while others questioned the morality of signing a player at such a tender age.

We can't see what all the fuss is about. Until this youngster came along, we were starting to rue the demise of the wonder-kid. You see, when we were young, they were all the rage – a *Newsround* staple, along with those ruddy giant pandas.

To us, the original wonder-kid was the Vietnamese boat-boy, Hung Dang. His family had arrived in Taunton in the late 1970s after fleeing the Communist regime in North Vietnam. Hung Dang shot to fame after winning a skills competition held by the Bobby Charlton Soccer School. His prize was to display his skills in front of 40,000 at Old Trafford. Dang's story was remarkable – he and his family had spent months adrift on the South China Sea, before a further spell in a refugee camp in Hong Kong. The story of the Vietnamese boat-people was a regular on *John Craven's Newsround* in the late '70s, making Hung Dang's tale even more poignant.

Hung Dang signed schoolboy forms with Spurs and even made an appearance on *Saturday Superstore* teaming up with Mike Read and John Craven. Dang attended the National Centre of Excellence at Lilleshall, and even represented England at under-16 level, playing against Denmark in the match that preceded the Mercantile Credit Football League centenary game between a Football League representative side and a Rest of the World XI. Hung Dang scored both England's goals in a 2-0 win over Denmark, playing in an England side that included Andy Cole and Ian Walker.

Unfortunately, Hung Dang suffered a stress fracture to his spine that brought a premature end to his professional career. He returned home to Taunton, recovering sufficiently to play football at local level. We'll never know how far Hung Dang would've progressed, but he was an inspiration for all of us. His remarkable journey even inspired a story in *Roy of the Rovers* – in the summer of 1986, former Vietnamese boat-boy, Pak Soon, made his Melchester debut – a fitting tribute for Hung Dang.

Sonny Pike was the next boy wonder John Craven brought to our attention. Pike's story was prime *Newsround* material. At the age of seven, he was invited to join Ajax's famous youth academy. It didn't work out as planned and Sonny quit football altogether a few years later. Pike went on to study psychology at Dundee University and started to enjoy his football again, playing in the local Sunday league.

Next off the conveyor belt was Freddy Adu, the Ghanaian-born sensation. Adu moved from Tema to Washington DC as an eight-year-old after his mother won the Green Card lottery. At the age of fourteen he became one of the youngest ever American athletes to sign a professional contract when he joined DC United as the number one pick in the 2004 MLS SuperDraft (whatever that might be). Even more remarkable than his achievements in football was Freddy's ability to freeze time – he seemed to remain fourteen years old for an eternity.

In January 2006, Adu became the youngest player to represent the USA, in a friendly against Canada. However, to the disappointment of the world's media, he didn't make the cut for Bruce Arena's 2006 World Cup squad. Instead, Theo Walcott got the nod as the tournament's official wonder-kid.

In the summer of 2007, Adu joined Benfica for $2 million; the world's media hardly noticed, as by then YouTube had moved on to the next pre-adolescent football sensation.

From this evidence, it doesn't look like being tagged as a boy wonder is any guarantee of long-term success, in fact quite the opposite – the sheer weight of expectation is too much for many kids. Hung Dang, Sonny Pike and even Freddy Adu offer a cautionary tale. But, for young *Newsround* viewers, these kids keep the dream alive – the dream that one day it could be them juggling a ball in front of a capacity crowd at Old Trafford. And, for that reason alone we continue to, err, champion the wonder-kids.

Club websites

Look, we just want ticket information.

We don't want to place a bet. We don't want to subscribe to *United World* (even if it does give us access to exclusive footage of reserve team matches). We don't want a bloody club credit card. And we certainly don't want mobile wallpaper in our club colours (mobile wallpaper!)

We've yet to come across a club webmaster who subscribes to the 'less is more' school of thought. Instead, to actually get to the information we're after, we have to wade through pages of useless tat and avoid being clobbered by pop-up adverts that have somehow evaded our state-of-the-art pop-up ad blocker.

And, when we finally get to the ticket information, what do we find? Yes, the tickets we were after have sold out. Gobbled up by Platinum Club members. Grrrr.

Club Wembley

Comprising 25,000 tons of concrete and 1,000 tons of steel, Wembley Stadium cost just £750,000 and took just three hundred days to complete. Of course, this was the Empire Stadium and this was the Age of Empire – an age where, rightly or wrongly (okay, wrongly), we bossed the Australians about, rather than having a load of Aussie subcontractors dictate to us when our national stadium would be ready.

Old Wembley was both glorious and hideously outmoded. The stadium with its grubby, off-white concrete exterior had an air of maudlin, faded grandeur about it. Completed just days before the 1923 'White Horse' FA Cup Final, the stadium had been commissioned as the centrepiece for the 1924 Empire Exhibition – by the time of its demolition in 2003 it was a relic of a bygone age.

Built on the site of Watkin's Folly – a never-completed construction, that was supposed to rival the Eiffel Tower but ended up being known as 'the London Stump' – the Empire Stadium was originally designed to hold as many as 127,000 spectators.

Capacity was gradually reduced over the years and, in the 1990s, the old stadium had the heart ripped out of it when the terraces were converted to seats, reducing the capacity to just 82,000. The old girl was never the same again, as punters squeezed into tightly packed seats, often with incredibly poor sight lines.

Wembley was about more than just facts and figures, and it wasn't – whisper it – just about football either. This was a venue that had played host to everyone from Evel Knievel to the Pope. Who can forget Knievel unsuccessfully attempting to jump thirteen double-decker buses after speeding down a flimsy wooden ramp. We're sure the Pope's visit was just as memorable, although he was no doubt warned off jumping buses in the Popemobile.

But, above all, Wembley was the home of football. Pelé went even further, referring to the stadium as "the cathedral of football... the capital of football... the heart of football". Pelé was obviously hedging his bets. In marketing speak, Wembley was always 'The Venue of Legends', and for once you couldn't argue with the ad men.

It was as if the world of football orbited Wembley. With the possible exception of the Maracanã in Rio, no other stadium came close.

As kids, all of our football dreams centred on Wembley; only the finer details varied. Some of us wanted to score the winner in the FA Cup final, others wanted to lead England out onto the hallowed turf. The twisted kids, influenced by Evel Knievel, wanted to dress themselves in satin and hurl themselves down a suicide ramp on a 50cc Honda.

Then there's the actual memories. Images of Old Wembley form part of our national consciousness. There's 1966 and all that – even those of us not born when Bobby Moore lifted the World Cup can close our eyes and conjure up images of that famous day. The World Cup victory aside, most Wembley memories centre on the FA Cup final. We've all got our favourites: Charlie George lying on his back with arms outstretched in 1971, Bob Stokoe running around like a madman in a hat, Alan Sunderland stretching to convert a late winner for Arsenal in 1979. Even Kevin Moran getting sent off in 1985. Strangely, nobody we know remembers anything about cup finals at Wembley after 1987.

Somewhat surprisingly, for arch-nostalgia geeks like us, when it was announced that the Empire Stadium was to be bulldozed, we weren't that bothered. In fact, we welcomed the decision. The time was right for England to have a state-of-the-art national stadium, a stadium that would be the envy of the world. And for all the arguments about location, the national stadium had to be at Wembley – Wembley, after all, was more than a location, it was a spiritual home.

Even as the contractors squabbled and the schedules slipped, we still backed the new stadium. Although we couldn't help thinking they should've added another 30,000 seats, to make it Europe's largest ground.

Then, as the stadium opened its doors to the public the doubts began to creep in. The first proper game at New Wembley was a humdinger – a 3-3 draw between England and Italy U21s. Unfortunately, the showpiece cup final that followed between Manchester United and Chelsea was a damp squib.

We even started to doubt the look of the stadium. The arch is impressive and vaguely iconic, but despite impressive girth, it could never replace Old Wembley's twin towers. Also, during the course of Wembley's protracted conception, construction and birth, stadium design had moved on. The Allianz Arena in Munich is a far bolder design statement than Wembley. Subsequent plans to renovate Camp Nou in Barcelona also make Wembley look a little ordinary. Arch aside, New Wembley is just another bowl-shaped stadium that doesn't differ much from Ashburton Grove or The Millennium Stadium in Cardiff. We can't help thinking that people will look back in ten or twenty years and view the stadium as a missed opportunity.

Watching the 2007 FA Cup final on the box highlighted the problems with the new ground – the sheer number of corporate seats. The business seats form a ring around the middle of the stadium, (prawn) sandwiched between the upper and lower tiers of regular fans. This layout dilutes the atmosphere, making it that much harder for the real fans to generate any noise. If you're a gold ticket holder and you've paid ten grand for the one-off licence fee and another three thousand for an annual season ticket, you are probably going to be too sozzled on the free wine to care what is happening on the pitch.

We understand that the FA has to recoup costs somehow, but the number of seats for luvvies seems a bit over the top. The majority of these people don't *love* football; they simply enjoy watching it every now and then.

A feature in The Game section of *The Times*, published the Monday after that first FA Cup final at New Wembley, really got our goat. A corporate guest was asked to describe his experience of the new stadium: "I ate steak cooked to a very high standard and the dessert was spot on, too." Jesus H. Zamora – who goes to the FA Cup final to eat steak? Is this what we've become? No wonder English football is cursed. The corporate guest continued, "… seats in the arena were near the royal box, to the left, near the Manchester United fans. The seats were very comfortable and padded. At half-time there were drinks and biscuits nearby and after the game we stood in the bar and watched the fans filter out." The arena? From the cathedral of football to a sodding arena in seven years – geez, that's real progress. Still, we're glad there were drinks and biscuits on hand at half-time. We hope that some things are still sacred, and that those biscuits were Wagon Wheels, but we sincerely doubt it.

Further confirmation of the corporate sell-out came as England played Estonia in a Euro 2008 qualifier on the same day that the English rugby team faced South Africa in the Rugby World Cup final in Paris (see Counterfeit World Cups). It was widely reported that many corporate ticket holders skipped the football because they were in Paris watching the bloody egg-chasing. We're sorry, but football always comes first. These people obviously have more money than sense. It is not just vital qualifiers they miss – there have been empty seats in the corporate section for other high-profile games at Wembley. The FA needs to instigate a three strikes and you're out policy. If a seat is empty three games in a row, you forfeit your ticket, ten-grand licence fee or no ten-grand licence fee. These seats should then be made available at a reasonable price to genuine fans – i.e. fans of the teams on show. Obviously, it'll never happen, but we can dream. And we do. We dream of an FA Cup final, where 85,000 of the 90,000 people in the ground are fans of the teams involved.

It is not too late to save Wembley, but the FA need to act fast or the circle will complete itself, and – once again – the site will be regarded as an almighty folly.

Come clean, Peter Hucker

You remember Peter Hucker, don't you? He played in goal for QPR and wore tracksuit bottoms. He also tucked them in his socks. He wore them on the plastic pitch, but why did he continue to wear them away from Loftus Road? They weren't even proper tracksuit bottoms, just blue baggy jogging pants. Did his legs graze easily? Surely, he had enough trouble with his surname without wearing tracksuit bottoms at every opportunity?

Players have thrown all sorts of stuff into the crowd. Shirts are ten-a-penny. John Aldridge threw his boots in when he left Liverpool. Mourinho chucked his Premier League medal. But we don't recall Peter Hucker ever throwing his trackie bottoms to his adoring fans. Why not?

Did we ever see an article asking him why he wore jogging pants? No. These are exactly the kind of questions fans want answered. They were also the kind of questions that no sports journalist ever dare ask. These, and others, like:

Why exactly do you like Simply Red?
Why have you signed for that club? It must've been the signing-on fee, because you've got no chance of winning anything with them.
Why are you always injured, you lazy bastard?

If these questions were asked more frequently, perhaps players would take more responsibility for their actions.

The media also have a responsibility to point out to players anything that makes them look stupid. Bobby Charlton had his comb-over for years, yet he was never asked why? Similarly, think of all the dodgy beards, moustaches and post-match clobber worn over the years. Then, think how much more fun *Match of the Day* would be if the correct questions had been asked.

So come on, Peter Hucker – tracksuit bottoms, why?

Comic sans

This book is littered with references to *Roy of the Rovers*. This is because *Roy of the Rovers* is our bible, our raison d'être.

When we refer to *Roy of the Rovers*, we are not talking solely about Roy Race; we are talking about the comic he spawned. Racey's adventures had begun back in 1954, when he appeared in the first issue of *Tiger*. By the mid-1970s, Roy decided to go it alone. On 25th September 1976, issue one hit the shelves containing 'eight super football picture stories' and a gigantic wall chart – what more could your average football-obsessed kid wish for?

We're not exactly sure when we got hooked on *Roy of the Rovers*, but once we'd been lured in by the combination of comic strip action and 'Sign Please' colour posters, we were fans for life.

This was no case of misspent youth. Everything we know about life, love and morality can be traced back to *Roy of the Rovers*. People swear they can remember exactly where they were and what they were doing when they found out JFK had been shot. Well, we remember as clear as day what we were doing when Racey was gunned down by a mystery assassin – standing pale-faced at the door of the newsagent, sucking on some Spangles trying to restore our blood sugar levels after reading the devastating news.

Fortunately, Racey survived and his comic strip continued to teach us lessons in life. His wife, Penny, gave us the first stirring in our pre-adolescent loins (see Racey Chat). Then, in July 1986 we were rocked by the death of eight first-team regulars, when a pre-season tour to Basran in the Middle East ended in disaster (Basran's a made-up country, GWB, before you start getting all trigger happy). From this we concluded that most of the people who marched through London protesting against the Iraq war were readers of *Roy of the Rovers*, as they – like us – understood the folly of invading sovereign states without good reason. And finally, in 1988, when a massive earthquake rocked Mel Park, almost swallowing up players and spectators alike, we learned it was unwise to build a football stadium above some old mining tunnels.

But, as we said, *Roy of the Rovers* was about so much more than Roy Race. When we look back on the stories featured, they appear almost biblical in scope and ambition. For Samson, read Hot Shot Hamish – the man with the strongest shot in football. Hamish Balfour routinely burst the net with his shots and sometimes they were so powerful they went into orbit. Then there was The Footballer Who Wouldn't Stay Dead – acting out the resurrection on a weekly basis.

For Simon's Secret, think *The Six Million Dollar Man* without the chest hair, while Jorge Porbillas was The Kid from Argentina long before Lionel Messi was even a twinkle in his father's eye.

Other stories, like The Safest Hands in Soccer and Billy's Boots (see Billy's Boots) have passed into football folklore. But for us one story stood, head and shoulders, above the rest – Durrell's Palace.

As manager of the Western League side, Durrell's Palace, Dan Wayne was the undisputed star of the show. Every week he would assemble a team of misfits just in time to pull off a remarkable giant-killing feat in the cup.

And every summer Palace's ground would be sold off to pay the debts, leaving Dan and his cohorts just a matter of weeks to turn a patch of wasteland into a decent football stadium. Even the acquisition of a pop-star chairman, Beverley Diamond (who looked uncannily like Rod Stewart) didn't help matters.

Durrell's Palace was our favourite because – in the crazy world of comic strips – the story felt real. It gave us hope. At the tender age of eleven, we knew we weren't going to be scoring a last-minute winner in the FA Cup final, but we could still dream of running out alongside the likes of Ernie Potts, Milky Mann and Dan Wayne in the Western League.

Roy of the Rovers filled in the gaps in our knowledge – we learnt how to deal with both triumph and adversity; we also learnt that José Mourinho's strops weren't a patch on those thrown by Danefield United's Viktor Boskovic.

But, with sales in decline, in March 1993, *Roy of the Rovers* limped towards closure. Racey had survived an assassination attempt, a kidnapping and a terrorist bomb blast (remarkably he escaped from the Basran debacle with just a dislocated shoulder), but he couldn't dodge the bullet of falling sales. Roy lost his left foot in a helicopter crash as Nick and Shaun – supposedly studying for their history finals – spent the best part of a week careering around the West Midlands trying to hunt down a copy of that fateful, final issue.

And this is where we worry about the future. In the fast-moving world of video games and alcopops, how are today's youngsters going to learn about life? In a world without *Roy of the Rovers* who is going to teach them about morality? We're buggered if we know.

Born into the information age, today's kids would just laugh at the prospect of waiting a week for the next instalment of The Chocolate Bar Kid*. For us, it was the suspense that kept us hooked. There were few things in life that could match the thrill of picking up your copy of *Roy of the Rovers* from the newsagent and rushing home to read it.

A life without comics? That's no life at all.

*We're still waiting for that next instalment. The Chocolate Bar Kid featured for only one week in 1988.

Communal baths

Modern football? Sanitised? Too bloody right.

And just when you thought it couldn't get any worse, they've only gone and pulled the, err, plug on the communal bath.

Apparently, today's sophisticated professionals prefer a power shower or an individual hydro-bath. We're sorry, but half the reason kids dreamed of becoming footballers was that, once a week, they'd get to splash about in the world's biggest bath.

As youngsters, we went on one of those tours of Wembley. Yes, we got to walk down the tunnel, climb the thirty-nine steps and lift a pretend FA Cup as the Tannoy piped fake crowd noise into the otherwise deserted stadium. But did we go home and tell our mates about any of this? No we didn't. We were too busy going on about the gigantic bath. Apparently, it took three days to fill it. And you could get one hundred players in it – all at once. And fish live in it. And. And. And. Well, you get the picture, we were only ten years old.

Sure, as you grow up, your ideas about communal bathing alter a little. But frankly, we can't imagine anything more appealing than sharing a bath with eleven muddy, sweaty men. How are we ever going to tackle homophobia in the modern game if we can't bathe together? Come on lads, it's a bath. Nothing more.

The communal bath is part of football folklore. Just won the league title? Shall we chuck the manager, fully clothed, into an enormous bath? Nah, let's spray him with cheap bubbly as he's trying to conduct an interview with Sky Sports News. Pathetic.

The world has moved on. Modern footballers get their kicks downing champagne in hot-tubs accompanied by heavy-breasted glamour models. They might be happy with these developments, but we're not.

So yes – as the murky grey water drains away for, perhaps, the final time – those are the tears of two grown men you can see mingling with the sludge and the Elastoplast on the slow journey to the plughole.

Counterfeit World Cups

Look, there is only one World Cup. The very fact that other sports have to add a rugby or a cricket prefix tells us everything we need to know. Football is the world's game. Rugby and cricket are not.

A record 204 nations will attempt to qualify for the 2010 World Cup in South Africa. Only the ninety-one associate and affiliate members of the ICC can compete in the World Cricket League, which serves as the qualifying tournament for the Cricket World Cup. In rugby just ninety nations took part in the qualifying campaign for the 2007 Egg Chasing World Cup. It's almost as laughable as the Yanks and their World Series baseball.

Then there's the history. From the moment William Webb Ellis picked up the ball and ran with it, rugby could only ever be a derivative of the beautiful game. The football World Cup began in Uruguay as far back as 1930 (although the FA, in their wisdom, didn't enter an English team for another twenty years).

Cricket's World Cup wasn't launched until 1975 and then the first three tournaments had to be held in England because – apparently – no other nation had the infrastructure to cope. Rugby's record is even more shameful: Australia and New Zealand finally got round to hosting the inaugural Rugby World Cup in 1987. English rugby fans will claim that at least their team has won a World Cup in the twenty-first century, but frankly, apart from a handful of back-slapping rugger-boys, celebrating in the gastro-pubs of Putney, did anyone really care? Kids might have played at being Jonny Wilkinson for a couple of days after the 2003 final, but they were soon back in the playground pretending to be Becks or Ronaldinho.

It doesn't matter how other sports market themselves, there will only ever be one World Cup.

Cramp or childbirth? You decide

Oh, the number of evenings we've spent chewing the fat on this one. Now we're going to throw it out to the general public, with scant regard for our personal safety.

In our humble opinion, the 'Wembley disease', cramp, is the worst pain anyone can experience. Ever.

With advances in technology, pain has been virtually removed from childbirth. The choice of available pain relief is bewildering. You can follow the earth mother example and get through the whole thing on a cup of camomile tea and some Olbas oil or you can go the high-tech route and choose between the Entonox (that's laughing gas, to you non-parents out there), a variety of epidurals, or just the humble TENS machine. If none of those take your fancy, or you're just too damn 'posh to push', you can always opt for a caesarean.

What assistance do you get if you fall victim to cramp while playing football? Bugger all. If you're lucky, one of your teammates might saunter over and half-heartedly offer to bend your foot back. Smashing.

Having suffered from cramp we just don't buy any of that childbirth nonsense. Allegedly, Katie Holmes got through the whole thing without saying a word. Try having cramp without making any noise – it's impossible.

Cramp versus childbirth? No contest. Just don't tell our other halves we said that.

Crowd segregation

For decades, keeping rival fans apart was an unenviable task involving a massive police presence, escorts to and from the stadium, eight-foot-high fences topped with barbed wire, CCTV and hundreds of stewards in fluorescent jackets.

These days, such draconian measures seem sooooooo twentieth century. The dawn of a new millennium brought with it a major breakthrough in crowd control. Someone, somewhere, discovered it was possible to keep rival fans apart with a four-foot-wide strip of plastic sheeting. Who'd have thought it? Ten years previously these fans would have moved heaven and earth to fight each other now they are successfully subdued by a few sheets of orange plastic.

We can't help thinking this method should be rolled out to trouble spots around the world. Who knows, perhaps the problems in the Middle East could be resolved with a couple of rolls of plastic from B&Q? It's got to be worth a try.

Cup upsets

2007/08 was the season that the 'cup upset' made a long-overdue comeback.

The first round proper, in November, set the tone with Staines Town knocking out Stockport County on penalties. This was just a taster of things to come.

Chasetown became the lowest-ranked side ever to reach the third round of the cup when substitute Danny Smith headed home a last-gasp winner to secure victory over Port Vale, this after The Scholars had drawn 1-1 at Vale Park. Unfortunately, Chasetown's dream ended in a 3-1 home defeat at the hands of eventual finalists Cardiff City. But the drama didn't stop there.

When Rocky Baptiste scored in the 87th minute against Swansea City to earn lowly Havant & Waterlooville a replay at Westleigh Park, no one could have predicted the drama that would unfold. In the replay, the non-league side went 3-0 up before being pegged back to 3-2. Then, just as an equaliser looked inevitable, Tom Jordan (son of Joe) headed home to make it 4-2. Havant & Waterlooville survived late Swansea pressure to set up a glamorous fourth-round tie with Liverpool at Anfield.

Liverpool at Anfield. A nice day out followed by a comprehensive drubbing at the hands of Premier League opposition? Not quite. The Hawks took the lead. Twice. First through Richard Pacquette's header, then with a goal from young Alfie Potter (a lad who sounded like he'd been lifted direct from a storyline involving Durrell's Palace in *Roy of the Rovers*). Sure, Liverpool eventually raised their game but not before the non-leaguers had them reeling.

Liverpool had been on the ropes in the fourth round and they were dealt a knockout blow by Barnsley in the fifth. Over 6,000 Barnsley fans descended on Anfield for the game and celebrated like crazy as Brian Howard scored a dramatic 93rd-minute winner to stun the Kop.

The Tykes weren't done yet. The sixth round pitted them against the millionaires of Chelsea at Oakwell. Kayode Odejayi booked the Championship side's place at Wembley for the semi-finals with a goal on 67 minutes. The final whistle was greeted with pandemonium as fans spilled onto the pitch to celebrate. They were scenes that warmed the heart and reminded us of days gone by.

With Cardiff City and Portsmouth making the final, the FA Cup was at last free from the clutches of the big boys. It was so refreshing to see genuine fans enjoying their day out at Wembley. These were fans who knew it might be years before they got to another final – and they were determined to make the most of it.

This plethora of upsets certainly breathed new life into an ailing competition. There is only one question mark that lingers in the back of our minds: in the old days, the big clubs would always field their strongest teams for FA Cup matches; now they often use fringe players for cup-ties. Does this devalue a cup upset? Does it bollocks.

Curse of the official club calendar, the

Most of us have bought, or been given, an official club calendar. After all, they're an ideal Christmas stocking filler for the football obsessive. What no one seems to realise is… the damn things are cursed.

A year is a long time in football and you can pretty much guarantee that Mr November or December will have been sold to an arch-rival or picked up a career-threatening injury by the time their stint on the office wall comes round.

The transfers of Ruud van Nistelrooy and Ashley Cole? Nothing to do with falling out with the gaffer or wanting more money, just some bored graphic designer deciding to plonk their pictures towards the back end of the year. Pity poor Djibril Cissé, loaned to Marseille while out injured with a broken leg: the lad's picture must have featured in consecutive months in the official 2006 Liverpool FC calendar.

Deportivo Wanka

Deportivo Wanka, a Peruvian football club whose shirts are inexplicably popular with British five-a-side teams. Can't think why?

Devil wears Gola, the

He doesn't really. But if Lucifer had to choose a kit manufacturer he'd probably plump for Lonsdale. That Lonsdale is the brand of choice for German neo-Nazis is not the company's fault. They can't help the fact that their logo when worn under a partially zipped bomber jacket spells out NDSA, one letter short of NSDAP, the acronym for Hitler's National Socialist Party. In fact, Lonsdale have worked extremely hard to counter this image by refusing to supply certain right-wing shops in Germany and sponsoring immigrant and gay-rights campaigns.

In all seriousness, we should be applauding Lonsdale, and any other sportswear manufacturer brave enough to take on the adidas/Nike football duopoly. For years the big two had football and especially the World Cup sewn up. At the World Cup, most countries would wear either adidas or Nike. Prior to Fabio Cannavaro lifting the World Cup for Puma (and Italy) in 2006, the last winner not wearing the three stripes or the swoosh was Diego Maradona (Le Coq Sportif and Argentina) in 1986.

As it turned out, the 2006 World Cup was something of a triumph for football kit enthusiasts. Not only did Puma supply kit to the winners but the company's support for smaller football nations paid off. Fourteen countries wore Puma, with Nike managing eight and adidas just six. But a round of applause for Nike too; they eschewed the usual 'same shirt, different colour' formula by producing kits that reflected the football heritage of each nation.

There's no doubting the big boys' global domination of football but how far does adidas and Nike's influence really stretch? Are they the invisible hand that guides the transfer market? Was it just coincidence that adidas' David Beckham left Manchester United/Nike for Real Madrid and adidas? It certainly makes life easier as Beckham becomes the complete package, dressed from head to toe in the three stripes. Barcelona had an offer accepted for Beckham, but did adidas in any way influence his decision not to join the Catalan club? Bringing the saga up-to-date, is it really any surprise that LA Galaxy is another club in the adidas stable?

Beckham is not an isolated example. It makes sense that adidas and Nike's marquee players are signed to teams that share the brand. Of adidas' 2006 star roster – Michael Ballack, David Beckham, Damian Duff, Steven Gerrard, Kaká, Bastian Schweinsteiger, Djibril Cissé, Kevin Kuranyi, Frank Lampard, Alessandro Nesta, Lukas Podolski, Raúl and Arjen Robben – all played for 'adidas' clubs.

It works both ways of course. It will be interesting to see if Ronaldinho leaves Barca for another 'Nike' club or if he joins a side supplied kit by its biggest rivals?

One kit deal does seem to remain sacred. England continue to be signed to Umbro*, the same manufacturer who produced the 1966 World Cup winning jerseys. And don't they milk it? After a brief dalliance with Admiral in the late 1970s/early '80s the three lions and Umbro have remained together for over twenty years. We're not superstitious types but given England's performances in recent World Cups could the union be cursed? Let's hope not. We rather like the fact that the England team have yet to succumb to the adidas/Nike hegemony.

*Yes, we are aware that Nike have taken over Umbro but, for now, the brand name remains.

Doctor, doctor?

Injuries are the bane of all footballers' lives, from the pub player to the professional. In the past, clubs relied entirely upon 'trainers' to identify injuries and treat players. These trainers were qualified in one thing, and one thing only – administering the 'magic' sponge. To be fair, this treatment cleared up most ailments aside, perhaps, from a badly broken leg.

Now clubs have a plethora of specialists on the payroll including club doctors, physiotherapists, masseurs and psychologists. The intention is to maintain players at their peak and keep them playing regularly.

While this is the norm in professional football, sadly it is not the case at any other level of the game. Instead, the current fetish of visiting the doctor for every minor problem has left its mark on amateur teams all over Britain. The list of woeful excuses is endless but the bottom line is this – why would you ever want to rule yourself out of a game of football?

We are of the opinion that unless you are physically unable to walk, you should always be available to play. There are two things you should never do if you want to play football every week:

1. Tell your wife, girlfriend or partner that you are injured or feeling unwell.
2. Visit the doctor.

Tell your partner that you are feeling poorly and they will hide your car keys. Game over.

Go to your local GP with any sort of football injury and they will treat you with complete and utter disdain. By their reckoning any football-related injury is self-inflicted and, thus, a drain on valuable NHS resources. You would get more sympathy if you'd chopped your own arm off with a blunt hacksaw and presented the severed limb to them, wrapped in a bag of frozen peas. Doctors just aren't interested in your injury. Their logic?

You shouldn't have been playing sport in the first place. And they wonder why obesity is on the rise?

Should you visit the doctor with any sort of pull or muscle strain, they will tell you to rest for anything between one and six weeks. If you damage your ligaments, going to see the doctor is even more pointless. They will try to tell you to rest for months. Pathetic. The only sensible thing to do is completely ignore your GP's advice.

Our remedy is to start kicking a ball around the house at the earliest opportunity, as proof of your return to 'match fitness'. Convince yourself you can't play and you won't be able to. Even if that hamstring is still a bit tight come match day, just spray yourself from head to toe in embrocation (see Forgotten smells of football No.2 – Embrocation).

Of course, what you really need is a physiotherapist who will diagnose your injury accurately and actually begin treating it. But your doctor will only refer you to one as a last resort. However, it is perfectly possible to treat your own ligament injury – keep active and wear a bandage when playing football. Simple.

There are those in your team who will take the doctor's word as gospel. If the doctor says they should rest for five weeks, they will rest for five weeks. If that's the case, sack them and bring in a new player. Professional clubs should take the same stance. These days, how many players go through the season as an ever-present? Sure, rotation plays a part, but what happened to playing through the pain?

The worst reason to miss a match is through self-diagnosed illness. The most common is flu. Think back to your schooldays. You would invariably get flu once a year. Then you would wake up wondering what the hell had happened to your body. You'd have aches and pains all over, every hole would be blocked or oozing liquid. You felt like death. Worse than that, your aunty would bring you a bottle of energy drink, not the orange or lemon versions on offer today, but the fizzy mouthwash stuff. There was occasionally a silver lining, when someone bought you a football magazine. Sod the energy drinks – bring us another comic.

Now, think back to the day after flu. You felt a hundred times better. You promised yourself that you would get fitter and eat more healthily to ensure you never have to go through that again. You were recovered and you were ready for football.

So when one of your teammates phones on a Monday to say he can't play on Wednesday because he has flu, buy him a fizzy orange drink and tell him to f**k off. He deserves it.

Once you are on the pitch, defying doctor's orders, your partner's instructions and all logic, use your pain to drive you on. Don't take painkillers they will mask the pain and may cause a worse injury. The thought of winning under such adverse conditions should spur you on. If it doesn't, go and play badminton.

But, whatever you do, never use your injury as an excuse for a poor performance, because that just marks you out as a tosser.

Kids, don't try any of this at home. Not unless you want to be a winner.

Dog shit makes you blind

When you were young, finding time to play football was never a problem. But being allowed to was. Your parents would think that visiting Gran or going shopping, or being fed as a family was far more important than your impromptu kickabout.

By far the most frustrating reasons given by parents attempting to curtail a game of football were ones that were designed to stop you playing on the pretence that it was for your own good.

The easiest one to use was the good old British weather: "You can't play in that weather!" How many times did mums in particular use that excuse? When you protested, a follow-up explanation was given, "You'll get wet through" or "You'll catch your death of cold." Didn't they realise? That was half the fun. Testing your skills against the opposition and the elements was the ultimate in park football. Playing in a bog and getting trench foot gave you life skills that couldn't be taught – not even in CSE General Studies. There was also the small matter of honour. Winning the game, or in most cases surviving longest in the adverse conditions, gave an enormous sense of satisfaction, and earned kudos with the tough kids at school.

When it came to excuses parents would try anything. The best ones sounded like they were based on fact, but left you wondering if they could really be true. In this regard, dog shit was the anxious parents' trump card. "You can't play there, it is covered in dogs' muck and dogs' muck makes you blind." But there was always dog shit on football pitches. If that were really the case, no one would ever play football in a public space again.

What sort of dog shit made you blind anyway? Was it the white dog shit that evaporated into dust when you kicked it? That stuff was ace. Was it the spiral dog shit – the one that looked like the dog was walking around in ever decreasing circles when it did it? Or was it the cocktail sausage dog shit? No one ever explained.

The myth centred on a mysterious fly that lived on the dog shit, and given half a chance would burrow deep into your retina, sending you both blind and mad. This rumour was never substantiated. It was just thrown out there in an attempt to halt the mighty game of football. The brainwashing ran deep: kids would spot dog shit while playing and shout, "Watch out, dog shit, you'll go blind!" Soft kids refused to play until the offending faeces were carefully removed using an empty crisp packet, and flung into the hedge.

Dog shit was one thing, but according to your parents, you couldn't play football in certain types of clothes. Sunday best was a definite no-no. But by far the most flouted ban was the one on school uniform. You went to school primarily to play football at break, we all knew that, so to ask kids not to play football in their uniform was utterly pointless. In playground football, you didn't have time to worry about protecting certain items of clothing. It was all or nothing. There was no avoiding a slide tackle in case you ripped your trousers.

Then there was the thorny issue of new shoes. This dilemma occurred at the start of every term in playgrounds up and down the country. Your mum had just forked out twenty quid on a new pair of school shoes and she had made you promise that you wouldn't play football in them. These shoes were so shiny they reflected beams of sunlight around the playground, temporarily blinding any kids who crossed their path. But no matter how hard you tried to resist, both you and your mum knew they would be scuffed to pieces by the end of morning break.

We were lucky despite parental objections, we were the last generation able to bend the rules and play football at every available opportunity. In the modern era of 'health and safety', parents have no need to construct obstacles – the playgrounds are gone, schools ban any balls at playtime, and over-zealous caretakers or groundsmen call off games at the slightest hint of adverse weather. As a result, dog shit has been replaced by bird flu as the cause célèbre for over-protective parents. "Go to the park? I don't want you going anywhere near those geese, you're bound to come back with bird flu." Okay, Mum, whatever.

Dogs on the pitch

"Even men with steel hearts love to see a dog on the pitch".
– Half Man Half Biscuit

In the 1970s, barely a week would go by without a canine pitch invasion occurring somewhere in the Football League.

Many a dull 0-0 draw was brought to life by a crazed pooch trying to chase the ball and bite chunks out of the referee. So much so, that when you returned home and your mum asked how the game was, you'd enthusiastically reply, "The game was rubbish, but there was a dog on the pitch. It took the groundsman and three coppers to get him back down the tunnel, reckon it'll be on *Match of the Day* later!" "That's nice dear" was your mum's stock response.

But in an age where watching the test card was classed as entertainment, a four-legged pitch invasion was a genuine spectacle. Like a bottle of Blue Nun, a dog on the pitch offered brief respite from the monotony of life in the '70s.

It wasn't just dogs; there were squirrels too. And if you were really lucky you got to witness a hare streak across the pitch at breakneck speed before it disappeared among the advertising hoardings (it was always a hare, mind, never a rabbit).

For nature-loving football fans, the Holy Grail was – surely – the flock of birds that, every so often, would land in the centre circle during the half-time break. Now, that was a sight to behold.

Escape to Victory

Escape to Victory is the greatest football film of all time. If it weren't for the irresistible charm of *Mary Poppins*, it would, without doubt, be the greatest film ever made.

You have to wonder why people persist in making films about football. *Bend it Like Beckham* wasn't too bad – but then Hollywood had to get involved. They threw millions of dollars at football with the *Goal* trilogy, then proceeded to set the first film almost entirely in Newcastle. Have they not watched Newcastle United recently? Or was it supposed to be a farce?

Anyway, how can you top a film that stars Michael Caine, Bobby Moore, Pelé and Kevin Beattie? Oh, all right, and Sly Stallone. How many other football films have websites dedicated to their memory or retro-shirts that outsell lots of league clubs?

Not only does the film contain some of the best choreographed football action ever to make it onto the silver screen – whose heart doesn't skip a beat when Pelé puts that slow-motion overhead kick into the back of the net? He did it second take apparently; even the great man misfires occasionally – but it is also a damn good allegory of the Second World War.

Think about it: clueless officers risk the lives of the rank and file with a daft escape plan; the Brits do all the hard work only for some cocky Yank to claim all the glory by saving a penalty in the dying seconds against the demoralised and exhausted Germans. Not only that, the film was so spot on with its history it even recognised the invaluable contribution of the Commonwealth nations to the war effort – casting Pelé as Luis Fernandez, a Trinidadian whose mixture of skill and determination got the allies back into the game.

If all that wasn't enough, the film even had its own hide behind the sofa, *Doctor Who* moment. We've watched the film hundreds of times but have never been able to look as Kevin O'Callaghan gets his arm broken.

The only flaw, in an otherwise perfect piece of cinema, is the crowd scene at the end. The French fans invading the pitch to carry our heroes away to safety are quite clearly dressed in 1970s loon pants. That aside, *Escape to Victory* is a triumph.

"Victoire" as they say in the film. Just never – ever – let anyone attempt a sequel.

Exotic commentary

Everything is polished nowadays. Clive Tyldesley can be commentating from some far-flung corner of the globe and it will still sound like he's sitting next to you on the sofa.

How we long for those pioneering days of international commentary – commentary that was bounced off fourteen satellites and gave the impression that Gerald Sinstadt was sitting in a field of cicadas. The constant hum, combined with the heat-haze, gave the impression that you were watching something truly exotic – something a million miles away from the humdrum of the football league.

However, it is possible to recreate the atmosphere from those early days of satellite broadcasting. We recommend putting the central heating on full blast, turning the sound down on the television, and slightly mis-tuning the radio so you are listening to three parts static and one part commentary on the game. If the radio is covering a different match from the one on the telly, the results are even more authentic. And if your household has one of those clever steam irons, you can leave it sizzling away in the corner for that extra-special heat-haze effect. Alternatively, you could watch some footage of the 1970 World Cup on DVD.

Figurine Panini

Strike up a conversation about Figurine Panini with the luvvies who occupy the Club Wembley seats or sit in the dress circle at Ashburton Grove and they'll begin to muse over the relative merits of artichoke and tuna as a filling for their toasted half-time snack.

Begin the same discussion with any genuine football fan between the ages of thirty and forty and you'll descend into a hazy, nostalgia-induced half-world, emerging, hours later, determined to go up into the loft and hunt out that long-lost *Football '78* album.

Panini stickers were a playground institution. Their arrival was effortlessly in tune with the seasons. Unfortunately, not football seasons. They never seemed to be ready for the start of a new campaign. Instead, the first packets emerged just as the playground conker championship was reaching its natural conclusion. Then, you'd be about to ask your mum if you could send away for those last few stickers when the pre-Christmas cold snap brought an end to playground swapsies and had you reaching for your fingerless gloves.

There was so much to love about Panini stickers. From the moment you ripped open your first packet you were hooked. Come to think of it, the smell of a newly opened packet of stickers was so addictive Panini could (had they not been the moral guardians of a generation) have been lacing them with crack. Then, there was the familiar feeling of reassurance as your mate shuffled through his pile of swaps while you repeated the mantra: "Got. Got. Got. Got. Swap. Got. Got. Got. Swap. Got."

By the mid-1980s, playground dealing in football stickers had become the perfect microcosm of Thatcher's Britain. Kids connived, lied and cheated on their best mates just to get their sweaty little hands on that elusive foil badge. The playground was no place for the stupid or the weak. As the school term progressed the 'deals' became more and more preposterous. Some of the transactions made Chelsea's dealings in the transfer market look astute. £30 million for an ageing Andriy Shevchenko? A bargain – we vividly recall the time some kid swapped nearly two hundred stickers just to get hold of Stoke City's foil badge.

There were, of course, conspiracy theories aplenty. The most common rumour doing the rounds was that Panini deliberately held back certain stickers. This is something they have always denied but, round our way, it was damn near impossible to get your hands on a Liverpool or Manchester United foil badge. The other rumour was that different stickers were released in different geographical areas. Looking back, we might have made this up ourselves in an attempt to get our parents to buy us a couple of packets on day trips to distant relatives. The third and final unexplained mystery was – why, whatever you did, did you always end up with four or five spare Trevor Cherrys?

International tournaments gave us an additional opportunity to spend our pocket money. World Cup summers were always best. Although, a bit like the Trevor Cherry conspiracy, we always seemed to end up with far too many players from Peru or Honduras. Panini didn't just stick to major international tournaments – they tickled our fancy in non-World Cup years with the exotic *Euro Football* collection. You'd think it was just a cynical marketing ruse to get more money out of young boys, but it was more than that – Panini taught us stuff. We hadn't got a clue where Helvetia was, but thanks to Panini (and a bit of latter-day internet research), we learnt that Helvetia was the Roman name for a region of central Europe that roughly corresponds with present-day Switzerland. We also discovered that the facial hair worn by many of the East European nations was a good ten years behind their Western counterparts. And, as a consequence, many players looked like they were styling themselves on Mungo Jerry, long after it was considered fashionable to do so.

There were other football stickers. In the lull between Panini albums, we flirted with Topps' and Barratt's but mostly for the free gum and candy. Panini were the absolute daddy of football sticker manufacturers.

It is reassuring to know that Panini are still going strong. The cards are much more jazzy and we don't care much for the fake signatures that are scrawled across the front but at least one bastion of our tragic youth remains more or less intact. Every now and then, we waver in the queue in WH Smith's and come close to buying the latest sticker album but then we come to our senses and realise that we can get the real thing on eBay. *Football '78*, here we come…

Flair for hair

Think back to the 1970s and '80s – mullets and shaggy perms were the order of the day. A footballer's identity was determined by the cut of his hair. The further up the pitch he played, the more outrageous the coiffure. Throw in a handlebar moustache or long, prog-rock sideburns and you had the perfect rebel No.10, performing at a ground near you.

And that's what you had – a performance. Players prepared to entertain and rock your world. Players you could identify with. Players you could dream of becoming.

These days most English players have truly uninspiring hair. It's short back and sides, or a close crop. Look at Stevie G, Lamps and Rooney in the England team. OK, there are exceptions – Becks, David James and Rio all make the effort, but their image changes from week to week. The rest of the lads generally look like conscripts, ready to go to war, looking a bit lost in the midst of battle. Prepared to give their all, prepared to chase that little ball all over the pitch, prepared to do everything for the cause. English football needs more than that.

Look at the Latin Americans: they generally wear their hair longer and look every inch the swarthy Lothario. They use their head, with the locks flowing as they run, to make the ball work in mysterious ways. Look at the swathe of new talent from South America – Messi, Kaká, Gago, Diego. They all have one thing in common – a fine head of hair.

Similarly, look at the older generation of English footballers. Hoddle and Waddle – the mullet brothers; the Beardsley mop-top; Tony Adams' unkempt Britpop style; the perms of McDermott, Souness, Robbo, Keegan; the Afros of Regis, Cunningham, Moses; the long-haired mavericks, Best, Marsh, Worthington. And Brian Kilcline, who combined ginger facial hair and a perm long before anyone had heard of Alexei Lalas. Even Bobby Charlton's comb-over was a work of art. And wasn't football better for it?

You only have to look at the 2006 World Cup final to highlight the greater ability of teams with hair. The generally short-haired French team were outgunned by the fabulous coiffures of the Italians. The dark and broody Buffon; the shaggy-haired Pirlo; the Luca Toni mop-top; the Grosso curls. France never stood a chance. If only Thierry Henry had grown back his hilarious moustache from the 1998 Finals. Oh, the impetuosity of youth.

Flashy boots

£119.99 for a pair of football boots? You're having a laugh.

Don't we ever learn? Who was the best player at school? The rich kid who turned up to football training in the latest Man United kit and a brand new pair of Puma Kings? Or the scrawny kid, with the bandy legs and boots bought off the hanger in Woolworths?

Perhaps, at the highest levels of the professional game, the strategic positioning of special rubberised fins really does make a difference. But if, like us, you've got two left feet, then they just mark you out as a bit of a tit.

We remember when the might of the adidas Predator was unleashed on the unsuspecting world of Sunday football. It was autumn 1995, and the venue was a dreary Upton Court Park in Slough. Craig Johnston and adidas had launched the first Predator boot a year or so before and it had taken just over twelve months for the technology to trickle down into the very gutter of the beautiful game. You couldn't get any lower than Thames Valley League Division Six, well, not unless you lied about your age. But there, on the killing fields of Slough, were not one but two pairs of Predator boots, worn by the opposition strike force. Of course, we took the piss but, really, we were shitting ourselves. We'd only ever seen this sort of thing on *Match of the Day*. We'd like to say that the Predator boots didn't make a jot of difference and that we earned a credible draw. And, in one sense, that would've been right. They didn't make much difference; we lost 5-0 and the result would've been the same if our opponents had played in a curious mixture of deck shoes and hiking boots. But the sheer presence of such expensive boots on a Sunday morning signalled defeat for us. It also marked a sea-change in Sunday football. Before long everyone was paying a small fortune to wear flashy boots. We can only put such extravagance down to the house price boom.

At least Predator boots incorporated exciting new technology and had jazzy suffixes like Mania, Supernova and Power Pulse. What really distressed us was the rise in the number of people wearing brightly coloured boots.

We know the late Alan Ball pioneered this sort of thing years ago (donning his famous white boots for the 1970 Charity Shield) but there should be a law against spotty seventeen-year-old kids turning up in them on a Sunday morning.

If you are Cristiano Ronaldo, you can probably get away with it. If you are a trainee car mechanic called Aaron or Tyler then it would probably be best to avoid drawing attention to yourself by wearing electric-blue football boots. Take it from us, it just gives ageing, thirty-something hatchet men something to aim for.

On reflection, we might be being a tad harsh on the youth of today. As we found out on a trip to our local, out-of-town, sports megastore, it is bloody impossible to buy a pair of regulation black football boots these days. We ended up with a couple of pairs of dark obsidian* boots, and not a lot of change out of £250. We should've gone to Woolworths.

*Look, we thought they were black. It was only when we got home and checked the dictionary that we found out that obsidian is actually a volcanic glass, similar to granite, usually dark but transparent in thin pieces. Well, you couldn't make it up.

Flip-flops

These guys earn thousands of pounds a week; they drive expensive cars; they date glamour models and pop-stars; they party in exclusive clubs dressed head-to-toe in designer clobber. Yet they continue to let themselves be filmed wearing flip-flops and white socks. *Football Focus* only has to roll up at a World Cup training camp to find half the England squad strolling around the hotel wearing the ghastly combination of blue plastic sandal and white towelling sock. It's like the '80s never happened.

Or perhaps it's an elaborate in-joke? Like the time they kept dropping song titles into interviews. That must be it – it's a gag that will only reach a conclusion once John Terry is captured on camera wearing pink and green fluorescent socks and a pair of slip-on loafers. Classy.

Fledgling league tables

A few years back no self-respecting newspaper would publish a league table until the fourth or fifth game of the season. And for good reason. Why waste valuable column inches on a league table that states the bleeding obvious?

These days a league table is published on the internet or Sky Sports News seconds after the first game of the season has ended. Surely we could live without this useless piece of statistical nonsense? It's not rocket science. If your team won their first game, they'll be near the top; if they lost – guess what? – they'll be near the bottom. Publishing these premature league tables only serves to heighten the pressure on managers, players and fans alike.

Lighten up, if your team is bottom after the first game, it's really not the end of the world, there are another forty-odd games to sort it out.

Perhaps it's us who needs to chill out a little. After all, a fledgling league table gives fans of Everton/Manchester City/Portsmouth/Aston Villa* the chance to be top of the heap and, for a few weeks at least, break the monotony of the 'big four' (see Big four, the).

*delete as applicable

Floodlight pylons

Once upon a time, every ground worth its salt had floodlight pylons. Great big things that lit up the ground like a beacon, making it visible for miles around.

We never had any trouble getting to an away match at night, we just pointed our old man's Ford Cortina towards the light and drove. The glow emitted from these monsters kept whole cities awake and caused birds to start their dawn chorus hours ahead of schedule.

When John Glenn, the first American to orbit the earth, reported an alarming yellow glow over Europe, Mission Control just checked the *Houston Evening Argus* and said: "Roger that. Everything's okay, that's just Ayresome Park, the 'Boro are at home tonight."

With out-of-town, flat-pack stadia and tighter controls on light pollution, old-fashioned floodlights on pylons have been hunted to the verge of extinction in the British Isles. But all is not lost: they can still be found alive and well in the outer reaches of continental Europe. Former Eastern Bloc nations are a particular haven for the floodlight fetishist.

These countries seem to specialise in a menacing forward-leaning pylon that casts an enormous shadow over the stadium and is capable of creating an eerie sensation of 24-hour daylight for several kilometres in every direction. Great examples of the genre can be found at the national stadium Lia Manoliu, in Bucharest (get there quick, there's plans to redevelop the ground by 2010) or Honvéd's atmospheric Bozsik stadium in Budapest. But the Holy Grail for pylon fans can be found at Carl Zeiss Jena's Ernst-Abbe-Sportfeld stadium where four giant, steel floodlight pylons dominate the skyline for miles around.

With budget airlines offering great deals to the outposts of Europe, you and your mates could soon be basking in the reflective glory of some really big floodlights – all for the price of an afternoon at Stamford Bridge.

Football Special, the

With adverts featuring an InterCity 125, Jimmy Saville and someone who sounded alarmingly like Aled Jones howling, "this is the age of the train," you couldn't get more stereotypically 1980s if you tried. Unless, of course, the train in the advert was populated by *Spitting Image* puppets wielding mobile phones the size of breeze blocks.

These were the last days of empire. And that empire was British Rail. Sure, we moaned like hell at the time, but – what we'd do now to turn back the clock. Privatisation turned our railway network into a shambles it also signalled the end of the line for the 'Football Special'.

In a TV advert from 1981, Jimmy Saville somewhat optimistically extolled the virtues of train travel: "You hop on at one end, speed away safely and smoothly with room to stretch out and move about." Clearly Sir Jim hadn't spent an entire Saturday on a Football Special.

A Football Special (or "Footex" in trainspotter speak) was often nothing more than a glorified cattle truck. Actually, cattle probably got a better deal – at least none of their number were blind drunk and throwing up in the corridors (oh yes, corridors) at 9.30am. Upon reaching their destination the livestock were usually put out of their misery. The passengers on a Footex had to endure ninety minutes of torture, before attempting the same miserable journey in reverse.

You see, Football Specials used the old rolling stock that no one else would touch. That way a load of drunken football yobs (for that was the common preconception of the day) could smash up the carriages and it didn't really matter.

As ever, the hooligan element was overplayed in the media. Despite the popular terrace refrain of "You'll never make it to the station," the reality of the Football Special was pretty mundane. Throughout the 1970s and '80s, thousands of fans were ferried up and down the country by train without major incident. Unless you count being stuck four hundred yards outside Crewe station for forty-five minutes with no working toilet as a particularly newsworthy event. These unscheduled, unexplained delays happened all the time on Footex services.

Most Football Specials were devoid of simple comforts like toilets or a buffet car but there were exceptions, very odd exceptions.

On 27th January 1973 Burnley fans travelled to Euston for their game at QPR on the inaugural 'League Liner'. This wasn't just any old train. It included piped music, a cinema coach and most bizarrely of all, a disco. A disco? In the morning? On a train full of blokes? (Remember, this was the early '70s when women were forbidden by law to attend football matches). It didn't really happen, did it?

Whatever luxuries these League Liners afforded, they didn't last long. Soon, normal, shabby service was resumed.

Yet the very concept of a Football Special was ahead of its time. Decades before anyone had dreamt up carbon footprints, British Rail were helping the environment by transporting huge numbers of fans by rail. But moving football supporters around the country required spare rolling stock, additional train crews and slack capacity on the network. All of these factors disappeared – overnight – with privatisation. These days, the railways are run on such tight margins that there is simply no room for Football Specials. And why offer fans cheap transport, when you can get them to pay full-fare and squeeze them onto already overcrowded, existing services?

It's not just the rail operators. Most new, out-of-town stadia have been built with massive car parks but no accessible rail links. D'oh! On top of this, television scheduling has drastically reduced the number of matches played on Saturday afternoons, meaning less opportunity to run special train services.

So, that was the '70s and '80s. Before we knew it, *Jim'll Fix It* vanished from our screens, Aled Jones' voice had broken, the railway network had been privatised and football fans were forced off the rails and into the motorway service stations of Britain. Progress indeed.

Football's Maddest, Baddest Away Days

If you've had the pleasure of watching an episode of *Football's Maddest, Baddest Away Days* you'll understand completely. If you haven't, we'll summarise the show for you. So, sit back, pour yourself a glass of Châteauneuf-du-Pape, and relax as a camera crew spends the day following a minibus full of miscreants on their way to a match in Barnsley – toilet-stop by unscheduled toilet-stop.

07.45

Seven blokes stand bleary-eyed in a pub car park waiting for the final member of their party – usually called something like 'Dipstick' – to arrive. Dipstick has forgotten to set his alarm (more likely he can't actually tell the time). And we, the viewers, are treated to footage of him running around the house in his boxers, shouting, "Mum, Mum, where's me keks?" Meanwhile, back in the car park, Weasel is having his first slash of the day behind one of those industrial green wheely-bins. The camera lingers tenderly on a stream of steaming piss wending its way across the tarmac to the nearest drain. And all this before 8.00am.

09.20

They're on the M5 – at last – but not for long. They've only been on the road for twenty minutes and, already, they've done a crate of Stella. Now, everyone needs a piss.

09.35

Big Nev tries to cop off with the woman on the till at the Welcome Break services. The rest of the lads leg it back to the bus after a bit of a shouting match with some Birmingham fans in the queue for a KFC.

10.15

The minibus pulls onto the hard shoulder. Weasel needs a slash.

11.35

Back on the safety of the bus, the mild verbal exchange with the City fans in KFC has undergone a beer-fuelled metamorphosis: it has become a pitched battle against the full might of the Zulu warriors – which our plucky lads won. Obviously.

12.10

Our lads do a group moon out of the back window, for the sole benefit of the cameraman following in the car behind.

13.00

The van pulls into Netto's car park on the outskirts of Barnsley. The reasons for the pit-stop are threefold: 1. To stock up on booze. 2. Weasel needs a wee. 3. To discuss tactics. Tactics? No, they're not concerned about the team playing 4-3-3 or sticking with two solid banks of four, they're talking military tactics. You see the whole point of this trip is to try and seize control of a small piece of Barnsley. The lads are determined to 'take' a pub. This requires a fair bit of planning. Firstly, they need to find a pub. Ideally this pub needs to be empty.

13.25

After driving through the back streets of Barnsley, our boys finally locate a boozer. Apart from the barmaid, the place is completely deserted. The lads pile out of the van and into the pub. Once inside they order drinks and some crisps. Big Nev uses all his charm to chat up the woman behind the bar, while the others sing a few songs about "shagging your women and drinking your beer", well, at least until the barmaid tells them to shut it.

14.40

The lads make their way to the ground, stopping for a piss along the way. Any interaction with the local shopkeepers is done in a 'comedy' northern accent.

15.00 – 17.00

Our boys start brightly, leading the chanting, but as the match wears on the hangovers kick in and they become less vocal. When they go a goal down, Driver Dave says something poignant to camera like "a 726-mile round trip to watch this shower of shit". By full-time, most of the lads are slumped in their seats, feeling a bit ill. But there's still time for one last hurrah. The walk back to the minibus gives the lads one last chance for a ruck. Sadly, all the home fans are long gone.

21.55

All the lads have fallen asleep in the back of the van. Driver Dave finally gets his fifteen minutes of fame. He turns out to be quite the little philosopher: "They're not bad lads," "it's all about the craic," "they work hard all week and just need to let off steam." He's asked if he really hates northerners? Dave replies sheepishly that he met a girl from Doncaster internet-dating, and would quite like to move up there one day. "Just don't tell this lot."

22.30

The lads are back home. Just in time for last orders. They're telling anyone who will listen that they had the Zulus on the run and that they 'took' Barnsley.

Football's Maddest, Baddest Away Days is not all beer, rucks and toilet-stops. Occasionally, there is a feature on an old bloke called Ken who did his national service in Stranraer. Every other Saturday, Ken drives from his home in Basingstoke to Stair Park, with only his dog Archie for company.

We're pretty sure this is how the programme goes – although we've usually drunk far too much fine wine to be completely sure. Either way, it's inspired television. Make sure you check it out soon.

Forgotten smells of football No.1 – Creosote

It's early August. The grass is mown, the nets are up, but the pitch isn't quite ready. There are no lines. You wait patiently for the final piece of the jigsaw.

You know when the lines are down because you can smell them. You can smell them from beyond the school gate. You can smell them as soon as you step out of your front door. At last, the creosote has been applied. You can't wait to get out on the playing field, inhale deeply and expose your lungs to the heady smell of football. We all did it, didn't we? Well, at least until health and safety reared its ugly, contentious head. No creosote – too dangerous. But we were never injured by creosote. Stained by creosote, yes, but never injured. We were never unable to play due to the effects of creosote. No one has ever sued for creosote-related illnesses. You might as well have taken away the ball.

If you needed a pick-me-up during a match, creosote was always there. Face down on the touchline after being pole-axed? A quick sniff of creosote would give you that much-needed surge of adrenalin – you would feel alive again – ready to resume playing the game you loved. White paint just couldn't give you the same high-octane rush.

We can't help thinking Robbie Fowler was on our side. His 'white-lines' goal celebration was completely misunderstood. It had nothing to do with coke and everything to do with creosote. That would've been our defence, anyway.

Although probably on the list of FIFA's banned substances, we say bring creosote back. Football needs a little danger.

Forgotten smells of football No.2 – Embrocation

Walk into any football changing room and there is one smell that outperforms all others (no mean feat on a Sunday morning, after a Saturday night excess of beer and curry). It is the smell that confirms you are a real footballer. It is the smell that unites the park player with the professional. It can only be one thing: embrocation.

It has been used for every injury known to man and is guaranteed to get you through the game. All this, and it is perfectly legal. The list of ailments embrocation has cured is endless. From stiff necks to sore toes, bruises, swellings, general aches and pains, head injuries, muscle injuries. And, if you are a bit of a masochist, cuts and grazes*.

In our playing days we'd swear by the stuff, but even now we're not exactly sure what good it did. It did give you a nice warm feeling, a bit like spray-on Ready Brek. We even knew people who would apply it to their legs as a genuine alternative to warming up. As for the exact medicinal benefits, well, you'd probably need to read the label.

But we didn't really buy it for what it could do for us – we bought it for the smell. As you went in for a tackle, you'd get a reassuring whiff of embrocation and you'd feel invincible. Like creosote, it provided a nasal high. Even now, if we catch a sniff of it, we descend into fits of dreamy nostalgia. Hell, it made us feel alive.

Embrocation. Eight out of ten footballers appeared to prefer it.

* We are pretty sure the patient information would advise against spraying the stuff on necks, heads and open wounds. So do us a favour, and always read the label – and always warm up properly.

Franchise FC

"This is not America, sha la la la" warbled David Bowie back in 1985.

Thank God for that, otherwise we'd be invading countries in the Middle East on the flimsiest of evidence, building cities on a ridiculous grid system and relocating our sports teams from one side of the country to another. Oh, shit, hang on.

Let's be clear about one thing – the franchise system, loved by American business moguls – has no place in English football. But equally, with the benefit of hindsight, the town of Milton Keynes and the horribly monikered MK Dons do seem like a match made in heaven.

Milton Keynes is a weird place – an (acid) casualty of 1960s free-thinking and an unhealthy obsession with everything American. The grid system that Milton Keynes is built upon was inspired by the work of Californian urban development guru Melvin M. Webber, who coined fancy terms like "a Non-Place Urban Realm." As we see it, the theory largely consisted of developing a network of indistinguishable roundabouts on a grid system devoid of landmarks, leaving the motorist with no visual reference points and, thus, utterly confused. The theory works on the assumption that the motorist will be so demoralised trying to escape Milton Keynes' clutches that they will simply give up and become permanent residents. Or something.

With its concrete cows and never-ending shopping mall the term, "Non-Place Urban Realm" sounds bang on the money. The only thing that prevented Milton Keynes from completing its metamorphosis from sleepy, rural idyll – yes, somewhere amidst all the tinted glass and concrete lies Milton Keynes Village (Middleton), a settlement that is referenced in The Domesday Book – to a replica of a town in the American mid-West, was a major league sports franchise.

That wish was granted in September 2003 when Wimbledon

FC moved into the National Hockey Stadium in Milton Keynes. The demise of Wimbledon FC – FA Cup winners in 1988 – has been well documented and still provokes outrage among football fans to this day.

Quite simply, you can't abandon over one hundred years of history and move a club sixty miles up the road. Better to die and be reborn like an Aldershot Town or a Bradford Park Avenue than to be relocated and rebranded like the MK Dons.

It is easy to point the finger at the opportunist businessmen that circle football clubs like vultures – they have no moral obligation to do anything but make money. No, the blame for the Wimbledon debacle lies firmly on the shoulders of the football authorities. They allowed it to happen. After all, moving a football club lock, stock and smoking barrel out of its community was against league rules.

But on the 28th May 2002 an independent commission ruled that Wimbledon FC could relocate to Milton Keynes. It goes down in history as the day Wimbledon died, and the day that the hideous American franchise system claimed its first victory on UK soil.

Not only had Wimbledon lost its club, but Milton Keynes had been fast-tracked up the pyramid system. The town had football teams in the past: Milton Keynes City existed between 1974 and 1985, resurfacing again in 1998 only to close in 2003, and there are plenty of other clubs within the borough that play at a decent level in non-league football. But it was out of the question to nurture and develop an existing club through the system. This is America after all. Success must be instant and it can be bought.

Another real tragedy of the franchise process was that while MK Dons were busy building a new stadium to the south of the town, Wolverton Park, once home to Milton Keynes City and also the site of Britain's oldest surviving wooden grandstand (dating back to 1885) was redeveloped for housing. Out with the old, in with the new, as the saying goes.

Of course, in hindsight things don't look so bad. Fans of the old Wimbledon established AFC Wimbledon and are now enjoying the autonomy of running their own club on their own terms. They are also making good progress up the non-league ladder. In contrast, MK Dons have moved from the National Hockey Stadium to a purpose-built arena next door to a supermarket and a purveyor of flat-pack furniture. This move is something we find quite considerate: putting three venues that we'd rather not visit on a Saturday afternoon together, in one handy location.

One day the two teams will meet, either in a cup competition or league, and we can only envisage a dramatic *Escape to Victory* style triumph. Perhaps Sly Stallone will arrive just in time to save a controversial injury-time penalty for AFC.

Until that day – like all football fans that deplore franchising, roundabouts and concrete cows – we'll give Milton Keynes and its football franchise a wide berth.

Franz Thijssen's indestructible balls

Franz Thijssen – UEFA Cup winner in 1981 with Ipswich, fourteen caps for Holland, 593 career appearances. A distinguished player, yet one who never quite managed to escape Arnold Muhren's shadow.

In the early '80s, only the top sports stars managed to attain highly paid sponsorship and advertising deals. Think Kevin Keegan and Brut or Brian Clough and Shredded Wheat. And, despite being part of the great Ipswich team of the era, Franz – unlike a number of his colleagues – was even overlooked for a role in the greatest film ever made, *Escape to Victory* (see Escape to Victory).

But Franz got his fifteen minutes of fame. His greatest achievement was the endorsement of an indestructible ball. It came in a cardboard box with the ball on show. On one side was Franz's face and on the other a picture of a ball with a pair of scissors stuck in it. Sacrilege, surely?

It was claimed that the ball would survive anything – scissors, a vicious knife attack, global Armageddon – and you'd still be able to play with it.

It was not an inflated football as we knew it. It is hard to explain exactly what it was. It was plastic, but spongy and thick. Unlike the leather balls around at the time, it did not get heavy in the rain. However, if you struck it hard enough it would fly through the air with an indent in it, which would slowly, after a period of about five minutes, rectify itself. It would collapse under a hard tackle but re-inflate … eventually. The bounce was low and it was hard to swerve.

We both had one, and they lasted a long, long time. We still played with it when it was split a third of the way round. It is one of the few things in life that we've bought that has outstripped our expectations. It wasn't a football in the purest sense, but it did its job. In addition to the scissors, the ball proved it could survive gorse bushes and hot car exhausts. All this, and yet Franz was the only man brave enough to put his name to it.

Would a footballer endorse such a product today? Probably not. Image is everything. A safe bet is a crap computer game, of which there are too many to mention. At least Franz put his balls on the line.

Free-kicks

Referees. Sort it out. A free-kick is just that – a free kick. How come we regularly see balls struck by the free-kick taker charged down by a defender only two yards away? For f**k's sake ref, blow your whistle and order a retake.

We are sure David Beckham or Juninho Pernambucano do not practise free-kicks for hours on end with an annoying little twat running at them before they've even struck the ball.

The authorities don't even moan about it. Thanks to Hoddle, Pearce, Barnes and Becks, free-kicks and set plays have been the most reliable (only, anyone?) method of scoring for England for years. If FIFA had taken a really hard line on this, England would have won the 1990 World Cup. Little Paul Parker wouldn't have been allowed to charge forward and deflect Brehme's free-kick over Shilts and into the net in the semi-final against Germany.

Blatter, as loyal subjects, we await your judgement. We won't hold our breath. Just maybe, it will be that old dead-ball specialist, Michel Platini who will give us what we want.

G-Force

Like the mighty G-Force before them, the members of the G-14 have hung up their spandex jump suits for good. In the cult '80s cartoon series *Battle of the Planets*, G-Force were the self-styled 'Guardians of Space'. They also cornered the market in natty feathered capes. In much the same way, the G-14 long considered themselves the 'Guardians of Football'.

Forget the *Battle of the Planets* analogy for a moment; the G-14 were more like the Bilderberg Group of world football. They called themselves a 'European Economic Interest Group' and according to their website they aimed to "find a constructive way of reforming a system in which their voice was not heard and to establish for the clubs a meaningful executive role in the management of the international game." Which, in plain English, seemed a bit like "sidestepping FIFA and making damn sure they get all the money from television and sponsorship." Or something.

They may, or may not, have been the sinister invisible hand controlling world football but they did have a delicious sense of irony – they continually refused to let the world's richest club, Chelsea, join the party. A classic case of new money versus old.

Then, out of the blue, in January 2008, it was announced that the G-14 was disbanding, its members absorbed into the 100-member strong European Club Association. Crucially the European Club Association is backed by both FIFA and UEFA, significantly reducing the threat of a breakaway European super league. Lawsuits have been dropped, flesh has been pressed and agreements have been reached – but at what price?

Perhaps the G-14 insisted Sepp squeeze into an ill-fitting 7-Zark-7 costume and perform menial tasks at all future meetings (to the uninitiated, 7-Zark-7 was the *Battle of the Planets* equivalent of Dusty Bin, only with antennae). The day we see the Phoenix spaceship parked outside FIFA headquarters in Zurich we'll know for sure.

G-14 members: Liverpool, Manchester United, Olympique de Marseille, Paris Saint-Germain, Bayern Munich, Borussia Dortmund, A.C. Milan, Internazionale, Juventus, Ajax, PSV, Porto, Barcelona, Real Madrid, Arsenal, Olympique Lyonnais, Bayer Leverkusen, Valencia.

Vaguely interesting fact: the last club to win the European Cup/Champions League who were not members of G-14 was Red Star Belgrade in 1991.

Gerrard final, the

Make no mistake, on 13th May 2006, Steven Gerrard single-handedly saved the FA Cup.

Often regarded as the greatest cup competition in the world, the FA Cup had gone into seemingly irreversible decline in the 1990s – a result of the increased financial riches on offer in the Premiership and the Champions League. Events reached a nadir in 1999/2000 when the FA Cup holders, Manchester United, refused to defend the cup, electing instead to fly to Brazil and take part in the inaugural FIFA Club World Championship. Two years later, with Wembley demolished, the FA Cup final moved to Cardiff and any romance was discarded on the hard shoulder of the M4.

It was not just the emergence of the Premiership and the expansion of the Champions League that threatened the popularity of the FA Cup – cup finals just weren't exciting any more. The 1990s suffered from a run of particularly dull finals, as anyone who sat through Arsenal versus Sheffield Wednesday in 1993 would willingly testify. But perhaps the biggest factor behind the FA Cup final losing its shine was television. Before Sky and the Premiership, the FA Cup final was one of only a handful of games that was shown live on the telly. It was a whole-day event. You'd settle down in front of the television at 9.00am and flick back and forth between BBC and ITV, watching a build-up that usually involved the players eating breakfast in their hotel before they – accompanied by an excited Gerald Sinstadt – boarded the team bus for Wembley. Stan Boardman or Little and Large would also be on hand to lighten the mood with some football-related comedy japes. In 1987, even Garry Mabbutt got in on the act, spooning an own goal off his knee into the Tottenham net.

It wasn't that the cup finals of the 1970s and '80s were any more or less exciting than their '90s counterparts. They were simply more memorable because they were the only live matches we got to see. We all remember Trevor Brooking's headed goal or Ricky Villa's mazy dribble because everything stopped for the cup final. In the 1970s, High Streets would be deserted apart from a few poor souls huddled by the window of Rumbelows trying to catch the game through the glass. These days the world carries on and the FA Cup final is just another live game.

However, Steven Gerrard may just have thrown the FA Cup a lifeline. He became only the second player in the history of the competition to have a final named after him. Stanley Matthews was the first in 1953, when he inspired Blackpool to a dramatic 4-3 extra-time win over Bolton. Gerrard's contribution was no less emphatic. He scored two and set up the other as Liverpool came from 0-2 and 1-3 down to draw with West Ham and win the 2006 FA Cup on penalties. Liverpool versus West Ham United was one of the greatest finals in FA Cup history, and Gerrard's 91st-minute equaliser was one of the competition's greatest and most dramatic goals. There might just be a bit of life in the old dog yet.

Grandstand's vidiprinter and the space-time continuum

Grandstand may be gone, but the vidiprinter lingers on.

Sure, it's only a matter of time before Steve Jobs and the guys at Apple shrink it down, give it a sexy makeover and put it in the palm of your hand – but until that day arrives the humble vidiprinter stands alone, a constant reminder of a bygone age.

The thing is, for all the recent technological advances, the vidiprinter still does the job. At the end of the 1960s, NASA got men to the moon on a spacecraft powered by little more than a prototype ZX Spectrum. Technology has advanced beyond recognition in the last thirty years, and yet they've not set foot on the moon since. Similarly, for all today's whizzy television graphics, nothing does the job quite as well as the humble vidiprinter.

We may be doing vidiprinter technology a disservice. Every week our team's result is typed out letter-by-agonising-letter. Then, as the all important digit – the digit that indicates whether our team has won, drawn or lost – is about to be revealed, the little cursor hangs there for all eternity. What we haven't quite grasped is the archaic vidiprinter's ability to bend the space-time continuum. Either that, or it just enjoys toying with us, as the longer the wait, the greater the likelihood our team has conceded two late goals, turning a 1-0 victory into a 1-2 defeat.

We also love the fact that if any team scores 6 (SIX) goals or more, the vidiprinter has to display the score in both numbers and letters. It's as if we'd think the machine had developed a dangerous malfunction, that, left unchecked, could spread to similar computers in the Pentagon and leave the world on the verge of Armageddon, like a modern-day Able Archer.

Another popular Saturday afternoon pastime is guessing the acronym that precedes the scores. As kids we were bemused by things like 'APL'. Were they referring to the Alliance Premier

League, the Athenian Premier League or the Applied Physics League (there they go, bending space and time again)? Sadly, we were never that motivated to find out.

We also lived in hope of the bloke operating the vidiprinter losing the plot (it had to be a bloke; no woman could be that anally retentive). How we wished he'd made up his own scores, or added satirical comment to the proceedings. Imagine, if you will, George Graham's Arsenal at the height of their 1-0 dourness, on the receiving end of some mild vidiprinter anarchy: Boring Arsenal 1 (Yes, ONE) Coventry City 0. Oh, the laughs we could've had.

Still, we are just grateful that the vidiprinter has stood the test of time. It's also nice to see that it still gets a few non-football jobs. For years, Mulder and Scully used vidiprinter technology to tell us, letter-by-letter, the whereabouts of the latest extra-terrestrial incident. Sometimes, there's just no better way of disseminating information.

Grass

There's a time and a place for grass on a football pitch. And, according to ancient law* that time was August. Groundsmen were allowed to lovingly tend their pitches every summer to ensure that the first three or four games of every season were played on an immaculate carpet of green. Then, come the first week of September, the ancient charter insisted that groundstaff drove a ruddy great big tractor over the pitch until the surface resembled a ploughed field crossed with the dark side of the moon. The pitch could then be left untouched until the end of the season.

Of course, this state of affairs had many knock-on effects. It created a, ahem, level playing field. During the 1970s, there were six different winners of the First Division. If further proof were needed, Derby County won the league twice in that period (1971/72 and 1974/75) and it is impossible to think of the Baseball Ground in the 1970s without recalling an ever-present sea of mud.

It wasn't just the League: the muddy pitches of the 1970s also contributed to one of the greatest FA Cup shocks of all time. Thanks to the presence of the *Match of the Day* cameras at Edgar Street in January 1972, Ricky George's equaliser and Ronnie Radford's extra-time screamer have become part of football folklore. Non-league Hereford United dumped Malcolm Macdonald and Newcastle United out of the FA Cup in a captivating third round replay. But apart from the Hereford bull, omnipresent sideburns and Radford's piledriver what do most people remember of the occasion? The mud. It was a quagmire even before thousands of Hereford fans invaded the pitch in celebration at the final whistle.

The lack of grass rendered skill pretty much obsolete. Can you imagine Cristiano Ronaldo attempting all those step-overs on a surface resembling a farmer's field? Would Chelsea's millionaires have it all their own way if they were weighed down by a couple of tonnes of mud every week? Football without grass sorted the men from the boys.

Greats were truly great, tested to the limit by appalling conditions. Legends like George Best or Stan Bowles adapted to their environment and found a way for their talent to shine through.

Once every four years, however, an entire tournament was completed on grass. They called it the World Cup. As youngsters we all watched in wonder as Pelé, Müller, Cruyff et al dazzled us with their silky skills on a carpet of lush green grass – grass made even greener by the dodgy contrast on our brand new colour television sets. It lasted less than a month though, and before we knew it we were back among the muddy brown sludge of the regular league season.

*Sadly, in 1992, the ancient law was repealed. Out went the mud, and in came evergreen pitches – perfectly manicured surfaces for the mollycoddled stars of the modern age. Things have got so ridiculous that some clubs will re-lay their pitch mid-season rather than have any of their precious little darlings come into contact with the brown stuff.

Great Duncan McKay bandage trick, the

Melchester Rovers left-back, Duncan McKay, was a defender from the old school. True, he looked a bit like Willie Nelson, offsetting his jet-black beard with a bright blue bandana, but never tired of saying "och-aye" and was as hard as nails. He was 'Big Dunc' long before 'Big Dunc' had raced his first pigeon, or barged into his first centre back.

Our favourite moment involving Duncan was during an injury crisis at Mel Park. Big Dunc was carrying a knee injury but Roy needed him to play. McKay would've run through brick walls for Racey but, to help his old friend out, Roy had a cunning trick up his sleeve. The plan, devilishly simple, worked on two assumptions:

1. Injured players are often targeted by the opposition.
2. Footballers are stupid.

Racey's plan was nothing short of genius. The plan was to bandage Duncan's… good knee! It worked a treat. All manner of fiendish attempts were made to crock McKay. Big Dunc was attacked throughout the match but, to the shock of the opposition, he rode all the tackles and Rovers won.

Quite why the opposition were so worried about a Scottish left-back was never explained. It was the sort of thing that could only happen in comic books – or was it?

Following this, whenever we saw a bandaged player on TV, we would always wonder if he was really injured or simply 'doing a Dunc'. Playing Sunday football, whenever we saw an opposition player with a bandage we kicked both legs. Just in case.

Hand in glove

Banks. Yashin. Trautmann. Look back at photographs of these goalkeeping legends and none of them will be wearing gloves. Before the 1960s, it was almost unheard of for a goalkeeper to wear gloves and if they did it was for warmth on exceptionally cold days. Gloves certainly weren't worn to give protection or to improve grip.

As the 1960s gave way to the '70s the use of gloves crept into the game. By the time we were at school in the late 1970s no playground kickabout was complete without some kid pulling out a pair of goalie gloves. These gloves were sold as a technological breakthrough, designed to turn a geeky nine-year-old kid into Peter Bonetti. The reality was somewhat different. The gloves were nothing more than a thin bit of cotton with what appeared to be bits of rubber from a table tennis bat sewn onto the palms and fingers.

In theory, this was a good idea: the nobbly bits of rubber would provide extra grip on that slippery playground football. However, the manufacturers neglected to tell you that within thirty minutes of putting on your new gloves, the stitching would come loose and the rubber bits would fall off, leaving you with nothing more than a brightly coloured cotton glove – precisely the sort your aunty might wear to church on a chilly spring morning.

We went through gloves quicker than we put holes in the knees of our school trousers. They always came in garish colour combinations: the yellow glove with black rubber or the green glove with red accoutrements were particular favourites. No matter what colour, they were all equally useless.

It must be so different these days. There's no trying to keep goal with a pair of soggy cotton gloves. Today's top keepers (and schoolkids) can sport state-of-the-art, waterproof, injection-moulded latex gloves that make their hands look three times their natural size.

Progress is all very well, but we can't help thinking it would be more fun to return to those carefree, glove-free days of yore. Or maybe we should leave Petr Cech, Paul Robinson et al alone in a room with a couple of table tennis bats, some old gardening gloves and a needle and thread – just to see what they can come up with.

Hand of God, finger of fate?

The greatest football horror story ever told can be traced back to England's quarter-final clash with Argentina at the 1986 World Cup in Mexico. It began something like this: Maradona. Hand of God. Wonder goal.

While that is a pretty good summation of our World Cup, the horror story here isn't about England's demise in that particular tournament or, indeed, every one since 1966. No, far from it. Forget about England for a moment. Does anyone remember the victorious Argentine goalkeeper, Nery Pumpido?

A non-playing reserve in 1982, he played in all seven of Argentina's games four years later, conceding five goals and recording three clean sheets on his way to a World Cup winner's medal. Well done. Story over. Not quite.

In a pre-internet age, the coverage of world football in the British media was patchy at the best of times, but Pumpido hit the headlines again in 1989 – in truly ghoulish circumstances.

Schoolboys across the country revelled in being the first to tell their mates of the fate befalling Pumpido. Thanks to omnipresent health and safety regulations and a nanny state, today's kids won't get to reminisce about a similar incident – they should count themselves lucky – the colour still drains from our faces at the very thought of it. Apart from someone receiving a blow to the nether regions, this is up there with the best of the worst football injuries you can get.

You see, Pumpido lost a finger – on the football pitch. His wedding ring got caught on a nail in the crossbar. You can imagine the rest. We have, frequently.

Hand of God or the fickle finger of fate? You decide.

Handbags, manbags and gladrags

There was a time, not so long ago, when all goalkeepers ran on to the pitch carrying a little handbag. Or was it a big purse? Shilts carried one, Clem carried one, even Big Joe Corrigan carried one.

The Goalkeepers' Union were clearly ahead of their time. Years would pass before manbags became the 'must have' accessory for the budding metrosexual.

Usually the biggest and scariest blokes in the team, why would a goalkeeper want to trot out on the pitch carrying a dainty little bag? More to the point, does anyone know what was kept in them?

We never actually saw a keeper delve into their bag. They dutifully took them off at half-time and brought them back out in the second half. Were they refilled with something during the interval? No one has solved this mystery. We like to think the bags contained something innocent, like some barley sugar sweets to suck on when the ball was up the other end. Or perhaps some lip balm to moisturise those chapped lips during the cold winter months. Or maybe just some signed photographs to hand out to adoring fans.

But given the amount of goalies feigning injury (think Dida or that Chilean goalkeeper 'hit' by a flare) we reckon it was fake blood, ready to administer in an Alice Cooper stylee, should the need arise.

These days, the keepers' handbag has disappeared and been replaced by the humble towel. Why? Surely there's not that big a scramble for the showers afterwards? One thing is for certain – like a priest in the confession booth, any goalkeeper worth his salt will be taking the handbag's secret with him to the grave.

Hot balls and cold balls

For some, the 'hot balls and cold balls' conspiracy is the biggest unsolved mystery in modern football.

For years, the rumour that the FA Cup draw is rigged using this method has been doing the rounds. Deranged fanatics have even telephoned *606* from remote parts of America to claim that the World Cup draw is fixed in exactly the same fashion.

We don't believe it for a minute but this is how it *could* work:

An FA suit, usually Sir Trevor Brooking*, empties a bag of numbered balls into a giant goldfish bowl. Two ageing ex-players then draw the balls out of the bag. One player drawing the home teams and the other the away teams. Here's the clever bit: prior to the draw, certain balls could be heated up while other balls could be frozen. The ex-pros are then instructed to pick a hot or a cold ball. This method could be used to keep certain sides apart or match specific teams against each other. The method is pretty much foolproof as not long after the draw all evidence returns to room temperature.

To us, this seems like the domain of the mentally unstable, but conspiracy theorists continue to offer 'evidence' to the contrary. In 2005/06 non-league Burton Albion, a club struggling with financial difficulties, were rewarded with a lucrative tie against Manchester United. The previous season it was cash-strapped Exeter City's turn to be thrown a financial lifeline with a home tie also against United. In these David against Goliath draws everyone's a winner. The small clubs benefit from a massive cash boost while the big boys have their path into the next round smoothed over. It is in the latter stages of the competition that things get really interesting.

In 2007, with the final returning to Wembley, the semi-final draw pitted Chelsea against Blackburn Rovers while Manchester United were paired with Watford. As if by magic, the FA got their showpiece final – Manchester United versus Chelsea.

Heaven forbid the return of the FA Cup final to the 'Home of Football' be ruined by the presence of an unfashionable club. Pure fantasy, of course, but it must've brought a smile to fans of Blackburn Rovers or Watford that the so-called 'dream final' turned out to be one of the dullest in living memory.

More worrying is the notion that 'hot balls and cold balls' is not a localised problem but a global pandemic. It would certainly explain why Scotland were always drawn against Brazil at the World Cup. More amusing though is the thought of Pelé frantically trying to work the microwave while Franz Beckenbauer coolly removes his balls from the freezer, backstage at the glitzy World Cup draw. Now, if only Panorama could catch that on camera.

*The FA is a fine institution, and in no way do we endorse these crackpot theories of corruption. Trevor Brooking is one of football's true gentlemen and we love him. He is also the only man ever to have successfully wedged a ball in the stanchion (see Stanchion, the), and for this he was rightly made a Knight of the Realm.

I was a teenage armchair
Honvéd fan

In the days before the omnipresent Champions League, European matches held an almost mystical fascination for young football fans. European cup competitions were also a lot easier to keep track of. First, only actual league champions were permitted to enter the European Cup. FA Cup winners went into the Cup Winners Cup, while a second or third place league finish would get you into the UEFA Cup (neé Fairs Cup).

The involvement of so few British clubs meant that you usually followed their progress even if they weren't your team. Of course, you hardly ever got to watch these matches. Only the finals were screened live and the highlights were on way too late for a school night. Instead, you listened to a crackly Ron Jones on BBC Radio 2 medium-wave, and, if you were really hardcore, you attempted to painstakingly recreate the match in question on a Subbuteo pitch spread out on the landing.

The key difference between then and now was that we had to use our imagination. Usually, we had very little to go on beyond the name of the opposition. Of course, we fell prey to crude national stereotypes: teams from behind the Iron Curtain were muscular, ruthlessly efficient and had probably bugged the visitors' dressing room, while Italian and Spanish sides were dark, brooding and prone to histrionics. But this lack of detail on our continental counterparts didn't turn us into *Daily Mail*-reading xenophobes – far from it. We actually fell in love with these exotic foreign sides. We all had our favourites although, if pressed, we couldn't really explain why.

People chose a foreign team for any number of bizarre reasons. Plenty of kids started supporting SV Hamburg when Kevin Keegan signed for them and many Liverpool fans developed a soft spot for Saint Etienne after the classic encounter between the two sides in the quarter-final of the 1977 European Cup.

But mostly we fell randomly in love just because these teams offered something different – a break from the dreary routine of supporting your regular club.

In a way, it was the football version of a holiday romance. You knew it couldn't last, but when an envelope with strange-looking stamps dropped through your letterbox you went a bit funny 'down there'. Supporting a foreign team was much the same.

Then there was the added bonus of the bizarre-sounding names. Think about it. You'd always go for a team with a stupid name. Ajax was an obvious choice, just for the 'comedy' potential of a name share with a leading household cleaning product. Smartarse kids would support Borussia Mönchengladbach – the really smart ones could even spell it. We're not sure what to make of the kids who professed to support Young Boys Bern.

Things got really interesting once you began to delve behind the Iron Curtain. We knew nothing about clubs like Hajduk Split, Torpedo Moscow or Red Star Belgrade (although didn't Billy Bragg have an uncle who once played for Red Star?). We were drawn to them because of their unusual names.

Once again, it was left to Half Man Half Biscuit to chronicle this unique aspect of social history. *All I Want For Christmas Is A Dukla Prague Away Kit* and *I Was A Teenage Armchair Honvéd Fan* referenced our obsession with obscure European football clubs while, at the same time, conveying a message of pan-European brotherhood. Probably.

Sadly, today's kids know as much about Real Madrid or AC Milan as they do about their hometown club. Gone are evenings spent hunched over the radio, trying to decipher snatches of commentary from Budapest among the static.

European teams are no longer shrouded in mystery or have that exotic allure. Instead, they are bitter rivals in a virtual European league. Chelsea fans are likely to despise Barcelona as much as they do Arsenal or Tottenham. The world has shrunk, football has expanded – and that's a crying shame.

Us? We still scour the papers for any mention of Go Ahead Eagles.

If the kids are United

This is the age of the oligarch and the American tycoon. Our clubs are dropping like flies into the clammy hands of foreign investors – businessmen who are interested in one thing and one thing only... a financial return on their investment.

However, inadvertently, one such foreign takeover has shown us that there is another way. The Glazer family's takeover of Manchester United provoked such an outcry among United fans that they decided to set up their own, breakaway club. Of course, AFC Wimbledon led the way in this regard (see Franchise FC) and, as such, Dons fans offered the United fans invaluable advice on setting up their new club.

The club, eventually named FC United of Manchester (the FA had rejected FC United as too generic), made its debut in the North West Counties Second Division at the start of the 2005/06 season. Playing their home matches at Bury's Gigg Lane, they drew impressive crowds and secured three successive promotions, placing them in the UniBond Premier Division (step three of the non-league pyramid) at the start of the 2008/09 campaign.

The club's progress on the pitch is impressive, but it is their off-the-field activities that make FC United of Manchester a beacon of hope for football fans everywhere.

FCUM is a non-profit organisation. It operates a one member, one vote system, as favoured by clubs like Barcelona. FC United's core values make such good reading they are worth listing in full:

1. The Board will be democratically elected by its members.
2. Decisions taken by the membership will be decided on a one member, one vote basis.
3. The club will develop strong links with the local community and strive to be accessible to all, discriminating against none.
4. The club will endeavour to make admission prices as affordable

as possible, to as wide a constituency as possible.
5. The club will encourage young, local participation – playing and supporting – whenever possible.
6. The Board will strive wherever possible to avoid outright commercialism.
7. The club will remain a non-profit organisation.

Source: FC United of Manchester website

The club even refuses to indulge in shirt sponsorship (the shirts themselves doff a cap to the great United strips of the past). For us, the FCUM/AFC Wimbledon model represents the future of football. Reclaiming the game from the moneymen, not bowing to the pressures of television, keeping ticket prices low and involving the local community are all essential if football is to serve any meaningful purpose in the twenty-first century.

FCUM have outlined their aspirations for the future, among them building their own stadium within the Greater Manchester area by 2012. The only dilemma we can foresee is that they become victims of their own success. Should they gain promotion to the Football League then they will face increasing pressure to conform to the existing football club stereotype.

We wish them every success, and hope they can retain their unique identity regardless of how high they climb.

Injuries

Players have always had injuries. So what is all the fuss about?

In the past players had a knee injury, an ankle injury, or a foot injury. Very few details were deemed necessary. Did anyone have a cruciate ligament injury before Gazza? Did anyone injure their metatarsal before Becks? As soon as a superstar has an injury everyone wants one.

Players used to disappear for months, without a clear explanation, which only added to the mystery. Players were carried off on a stretcher and you feared for both their lives and careers. When players are carried off on a stretcher today, they have a drink, wave to the crowd, adjust their tackle and return to the action as soon as the referee will allow.

If one of our players is going to be out for months we want to see the injury happen and be able to tell it is a bad one. We don't want to see him in the crowd at matches, at the races or on celebrity TV shows. We don't want him commentating on the radio, and we don't want to read about his progress in his bland ghostwritten column. We just want him fully fit.

So if you get injured, don't invite *OK* magazine round to do a feature on living with a broken metatarsal. Go live in an oxygen tent, train like Rocky and come back stronger – it will work a treat, just ask Raúl.

International friendlies

International friendlies are pointless. They are the professional footballers' equivalent of a duvet day. Half the team phone in sick, leaving the manager with no choice but to hand debuts to players who are never going to get a sniff when it comes to a proper competitive fixture.

This hotch-potch of journeymen and untried youngsters then loses to someone like Belarus or Austria, racking up the pressure on the already under-fire manager. Who, apart from the plethora of one-cap wonders, benefits from this shambles?

Here's our answer: scrap the meaningless friendlies and re-introduce the Home Internationals. Play the tournament at the end of the season in the years when there's no World Cup or European Championship. The opportunity to get one over on the English would be great for Scotland, Wales and Northern Ireland. And hopefully, the prospect of losing to our near-neighbours would foster a bit of national pride among some of the overpaid layabouts that make up the England team.

Come on England, don't be shy... ask nicely and maybe you can take part in the Celtic Cup.

Jesus Zamora

When is swearing not really swearing? When it's the Christian name of a World Cup star. The year was 1982. Wearing the number ten shirt in the Spanish World Cup squad was the Real Sociedad midfielder, Jesus Zamora. Aside from scoring a late goal as Spain lost 2-1 to West Germany, Zamora's impact on the World Cup was minimal. But that summer, he made quite an impression in the playgrounds of Britain.

For a ten-year-old, just to hear the name 'Jesus' on television was a revelation. As young boys, using 'Jesus' in any sort of exclamation meant a rap on the arse with a plastic sweeping brush. Think about it. Your Nan would go apoplectic at any sort of blasphemous outburst. But suddenly, she could be plunged into despair as you shouted, "Jesus … Zamora" at the TV. "It's not a swear word, Nan, honest. He's a football player."

Kids shouted it everywhere. And just like his more illustrious namesake, Jesus Zamora's name could be used to express a range of emotions: hit the post during a breaktime kickabout and a pissed-off "Jesus Zamora" would ring out across the playground. A wonder goal, just before the bell for the end of lunch and an awe-inspired "Jesus Zamora" could be heard. Told you have to finish your vegetables at tea time? Yep, "Jesus Zamora" again.

Apparently, there were two Jesus's in that squad. However, Jesus Satrustegui didn't roll off the tongue as easily, and he never achieved the same level of notoriety. During the heady summer of 1982, Jesus was our best friend. But like many childhood friendships he was lost with the passage of time. However, he pops up whenever we play the retro swear word game. You know, the game where two groups of consenting adults exchange childhood insults until one group runs out. "Jesus Zamora" never fails to raise an impressed "ooooh" from the other participants. At least until some clever sod pipes up, "Isn't it pronounced hey-zeuss?" We were only ten, how the hell were we supposed to know?

Reckon today's kids have as much fun with Danny Shittu?

Jeux sans frontières

It's a right royal knockout, this one.

'Game 39' – the Premier League's crackpot plan to conquer the world. How exactly are they going to achieve this? That's right, by hawking your football club around the globe, getting them to play an extra game in some distant timezone. What, Blackburn v Middlesbrough in Shanghai is not that appealing? Don't worry, they're not quite finished. How about dressing both sets of players in giant penguin costumes, and getting them to collect buckets of water while dodging giant foam icebergs? Yep, very funny. Only this time it's not just Stuart Hall dissolving into fits of laughter, it's the whole bloody world.

For once we don't need to rant. Apart from Richard Scudamore and a few club chairmen, pretty much the whole world rushed to condemn 'Game 39'. Within hours, fans were bombarding radio phone-ins, starting Facebook petitions and generally getting quite hot under the collar about the prospect of an 'international round' of matches. And with good reason: it's us fans who are being shafted. Even the great and the good were quick to round on the plans. Michel Platini called the idea "nonsense" before really sticking the knife in: "In England, you already have no English coach, no English players and maybe now you will have no clubs playing in England. It's a joke."

Meanwhile, Sepp Blatter snarled, "This will never happen, at least as long as I am the president of FIFA." More worryingly, statisticians the world over lost sleep, fretting over the extra column they'd be forced to add to their league tables to accommodate the 39th game. Scudamore needs to heed this warning. It's okay to mess with us ordinary fans, but don't upset a statistician. They'll hunt you down, and in the dead of night beat you to a pulp with a scientific calculator and a rolled-up spreadsheet.

Anyway, we're not interested in the sheer nonsense of 'Game 39'. You don't need us to tell you it's a ludicrous idea.

We want to know how they came up with such a bonkers plan. Who the hell is responsible for putting the idea into their heads? It must have come from somewhere? They sure as hell don't look like men capable of original thought. That's right – we want scapegoats. And we want them NOW.

So let's start at the beginning. Who's usually to blame for a monumental f**k-up of global proportions? That's right, the Americans. And, at first glance, it all seems to add up…

At Wembley Stadium on 28th October 2007 the New York Giants beat the Miami Dolphins 13-10 in the first competitive NFL game to be played outside of North America. For anyone who remembers William 'The Fridge' Perry thundering around the old Wembley some twenty years earlier, this doesn't seem particularly revolutionary. After all, in 1986, American Football was at the height of its (Channel 4 assisted) popularity and it still didn't pose a threat to the beautiful game. But in 1986, half of England's leading clubs weren't in the hands of foreign owners, and the money to be made from TV rights was paltry in comparison to the riches now on offer.

By playing a competitive fixture on foreign soil the Dolphins and the Giants set a precedent. More worrying was the talk emanating from the American sports executives jollying it up in London in the week leading up to the game. At a conference about the future of sport they hit upon the idea that a Premier League match could be staged in the United States. Then they started muttering about the possibility of a Premier League franchise in New York or Los Angeles. On the day of the Dolphins/Giants face-off, *The Observer* was quoting American executives coming up with gumpf like "Businesses are not talking about borders, that's the game changer here" and "Just think what's going to happen when India starts getting really active". Yeah, just think.

Let's be honest, most of the American television audience watching the Giants and the Dolphins playing at Wembley wouldn't have had a clue that the game was taking place outside the US. Ask most Americans to locate London on a map and they'd probably stick a pin somewhere between Arkansas and Idaho. But let's leave aside the stupidity of a nation for a moment. It's a cast-iron fact that American sports fans don't travel in numbers to away games. The sheer size of the country makes following your team away from home totally impractical. It's not like a load of Yanks are going to squeeze into a minibus and drive from Los Angeles to Miami to watch a game of gridiron. And this is the crux of the matter. International businessmen can spot a cash-cow at forty paces, but they don't give a monkey's about supporters or tradition. Why should they care about the fan who has followed his club home and away for the last forty years? If they can't afford to travel to Tokyo to watch a game, tough.

Perhaps it is too easy to blame the Yanks. If it wasn't the Americans' fault, then Formula One's petrol-heads must be to blame. Turn on the telly on a Sunday morning and there's a Grand Prix in full flow in some new exotic location. Why not add football to the global circus? After a couple of hours getting dizzy watching the motor racing, even Blackburn v Middlesbrough would seem like decent entertainment.

Worryingly, our search for a scapegoat unearthed an actual, bona fide precedent from the world of football. We're not sure the Premier League were aware of this, as surely they'd have been shouting about it from the roof top of their Gloucester Place HQ. This precedent has the lot – competitive matches played in a different country, serving as a qualification tournament for a competition on an entirely different continent. Confused? Read on.

It all started in 2004 when two Mexican teams were granted automatic places in the Copa Libertadores (South America's Champions League equivalent). The Mexican FA then created a qualifying league called the InterLiga to determine which teams would participate in the Copa Libertadores. Eight teams were then divided into two groups of four in order to battle it out. Qualification is a bloomin' confusing process that's not worth discussing here. It's also not worth contemplating why Mexican teams from FIFA's North and Central American region (CONCACAF) get to play in the South American (CONMEBOL)

Copa Libertadores. What is crucial is that these games don't take place in Mexico. The entire InterLiga tournament is played in the US. Matches are usually played in California or Texas, two states with a large Mexican immigrant population who relish the opportunity of watching competitive football from their homeland. So, perhaps, the InterLiga is the 'game changer' that those pesky sports executives were referring to. Just no one tell the Premier League. They'd like the idea even more if they knew that some of the games were played at the delightfully named Pizza Hut Park in Dallas.

Fortunately, as far as 'Game 39' goes it looks like we've got ourselves a Mexican standoff. The Premier League are cooling on the idea, while the rest of the world, including FIFA and UEFA, think that it is utterly bonkers.

As for a scapegoat, our search has taken us round the world, but the real culprit can be found much closer to home – just a short hop across La Manche. Yes, for this one, the blame lies firmly at the door of the French. If it hadn't been for Charles de Gaulle and his vision of pan-European silliness *Jeux Sans Frontières* none of this would have happened. Football needs boundaries. It's as simple as that.

Jimmy Hill

Jimmy Hill was one of football's true pioneers. He was certainly a man ahead of his time. Jimmy started his playing career at Brentford in 1949, he moved to Fulham four years later and went on to clock up more than three hundred appearances for the Cottagers. He even managed to score five goals in the 6-1 rout of Doncaster Rovers at Belle Vue in 1958. However, it was off the pitch that Jimmy really started making waves.

The late 1950s/early '60s was the age of the bearded revolutionary. Looking back, it is almost impossible to distinguish between the Balham-born Hill and the iconic Che Guevara. And we're not just talking facial hair.

As Guevara languished in the Sierra Maestra plotting to overthrow Batista's military regime, Hill quietly assumed control of the Professional Footballers' Association. As Che advanced on Havana, Jimmy's plans to topple the existing order also went into overdrive. In 1961, Hill succeeded in his campaign to scrap football's maximum wage of £20 a week (£17 a week in the summer). It was an era-defining moment. At last footballers were free to throw off the shackles of oppression and let the free market determine their worth.

It didn't take long for the effects to take hold: before the year was out Johnny Haynes became the first player to be paid £100 a week. As a result of his revolutionary activity, Hill's bearded visage was immortalised on T-shirts and posters that remain a firm favourite with students and beatnik weirdos to this very day.

Jimmy didn't rest on his laurels, mind. As manager, he masterminded Coventry City's rise from the Third to the First Division. Jimmy's vision is said to have included the introduction of a sky blue train to away matches (designed, one assumes, to match the newly introduced sky blue kit). Children were plied with fizzy drinks and free sweets, and extravagant pre-match entertainment was introduced.

But, ever the astute revolutionary, Jimmy Hill recognised that to control the media was to control the game, and he resigned as manager of Coventry City, on the eve of their First Division debut, to begin a career in television.

The giddy scent of revolution still hung heavy in the air as Jimmy began his job as Head of Sport at London Weekend Television. It was a timely move on Hill's part. In 1970, two things changed televised football forever. First, thanks to satellite technology, matches from the Mexico '70 World Cup were beamed live and – in colour – into living rooms around the country. Second, Jimmy Hill unleashed the first ever panel of pundits on an unsuspecting nation. While the BBC played safe with their coverage, over on ITV, Brian Moore struggled to control the likes of Malcolm Allison, Pat Crerand, Derek Dougan and Bob McNab. It was a televisual masterstroke.

By the mid-1970s Jimmy Hill was back at Coventry City, first as managing director, then as chairman. The visionary ideas continued as before. With a nod to the success of American sports marketing, Hill introduced the league's first electronic scoreboard. More controversially, he turned Highfield Road into Britain's first all-seater stadium, leading with the slogan "You can't be a hooligan sitting down." Unfortunately, even maverick visionaries like Jimmy Hill get things wrong, and the decision to make Highfield Road all-seater was incredibly unpopular. Attendances tumbled and eventually terracing was reintroduced. Of course, with the benefit of hindsight, Jimmy Hill seems remarkably prescient – by the mid-1990s all-seater stadiums were the norm in English football.

Jimmy was good, but he wasn't all-knowing. How much responsibility Jimmy Hill should shoulder for Coventry City's awful chocolate brown away kit from the mid-1970s we can't be sure. Then there was the apparent attempt to change the club's name to 'Coventry Talbot' to get round the television ban on their controversial 'Talbot-T' kit, which they wore between 1981 and 1983.

By the time of the 1978 World Cup in Argentina, Jimmy was a regular on the BBC's *Match of the Day*. But joining

Auntie hadn't diminished his thirst for new ideas and he chose the 1978 tournament to introduce the 'Tele-tracker' – a groundbreaking device that left something akin to the tail of a comet following the ball during slow-motion action replays. Viewers sat spellbound in their armchairs as they watched the free-kicks fly into the top corner followed by a trail of dandruff. To think people credit Sky with all the great leaps forward in television football coverage.

In between clocking up nearly six hundred appearances on *Match of the Day*, Hill championed the move to three points for a win, adopted by the Football League at the start of the 1981/82 season. Hill's system is now pretty much standard around the globe.

The more we delve into Jimmy's past the more he stands out as a man ahead of his time. From abolishing the maximum wage to understanding the power of television, Hill was a visionary. Unfortunately, come judgement day, none of this will be remembered. For an entire generation Jimmy Hill will forever be a childish playground riposte.

During the 1970s and '80s kids would scratch their chins and say "Jimmy Hill" whenever they thought one of their school mates was telling lies. Picture the scene. Kid A: "My Dad's new Cortina can go faster than the speed of sound." Kid B: "Jimmmmmmy Hill" (accompanied by exaggerated stroking of chin). Our research has concluded this was pretty much a nationwide phenomenon. Regional variations included the plain "Jimmy," the obvious "Jimmy Chin," or the hybrid "Jimmy Reckon." So ubiquitous was Hill's presence in the playground that you could get away with a "Chinny, Chinny" or a "Reckon" and as long as you were scratching an imaginary beard, kids from Dundee to Dunstable knew exactly what you were on about. This is Jimmy Hill's true legacy – "Reckon?"

John "would you believe it" Motson

Yes, Motty, we do bloody believe it. We've just seen it on the telly. And look, now they're showing replays from loads of different angles.

Motty – you are a broadcasting legend and we live in constant fear of the day you decide to hang up your sheepskin coat for good.

Jossy's Giants

"We're called Jossy's Giants, football's just a branch of science..."

Forget *The Dream Team*, or, heaven forbid, *Footballers' Wives*. *Jossy's Giants* stands head and shoulders above the competition when it comes to football drama on the telly. Central Television's *Murphy's Mob* wasn't bad, and *The Manageress* pandered to our sexual fantasies by casting Cherie Lunghi as a yummy-mummy authority figure, but nothing could top *Jossy's Giants*.

For a start it was written by Geordie darts commentator Sid Waddell. He got the idea for the programme after his son Daniel joined a boys team in Leeds. In the programme, a fictional team, the Glipton Grasshoppers, are taken over by new coach Joswell 'Jossy' Blair. Jossy himself had been a child prodigy whose career at Newcastle United was cut short when he was injured on his first team debut. Somehow, he transforms the hapless Grasshoppers into the mighty Giants.

Jossy's team was drawn from kids playing park football around Manchester. The producers thought it would be easier to teach children who could play football how to act than vice-versa. Those chosen to star in the series were so good that they knocked the cast of *Byker Grove* into a cocked hat.

There was Harvey, the goalkeeper, who had a penchant for astrology and ice skating. In one episode, he memorably skated out onto the local ice rink to Torvill and Dean's Bolero, and promptly fell flat on his arse.

Then there were the strikers, Glenn and Selly, quite possibly the only punks ever to play junior football. The real star of the show – and eye candy for all of us fourteen-year-old boys – was Tracey Gaunt (Julie Foy, who later went on to play Gina Seddon in *Coronation Street*). She was the Giants' voice of reason and her quick thinking frequently got Jossy and the lads out of any bother.

A host of football celebrities had cameos in the show. In

the first series, Bobby Charlton invited the lads to visit St James' Park, Newcastle. In the second series, the team travelled to London to watch the filming of *A Question of Sport*, bumping into both Bryan Robson and David Coleman.

What set *Jossy's Giants* apart from other football dramas was that – despite all the madcap plot lines – football remained central to the series.

In classic sitcom style, the last ever episode found Jossy at St James' Park (no, not that one) managing the Giants when he should've been at church getting hitched to Councillor Glenda Fletcher. A lot of fretting and one ambulance chase later, Jossy and Glenda tied the knot in the centre circle before heading off on honeymoon to Sorrento (via Newcastle to watch a friendly match between Jossy's beloved United and Inter Milan).

Jossy's Giants was, undoubtedly, the high watermark in football comedy. Ask any self-respecting football fan aged between thirty and forty; at the very least, he or she will be able to sing the theme tune. All together now:

"Dependable, reliant, put your faith in Jossy's Giants, get stuck in, we're gonna win... JOSSY'S GIANTS!!"

Jumpers for goalposts

Geoff Hurst's second goal in the World Cup Final of 1966 is probably the most contentious in the history of football. Players, pundits and fans still discuss it today – just imagine the furore if there had been 'jumpers for goalposts' at Wembley that day?

Before organised youth football became widespread and while children were allowed to roam free in the evenings and at weekends, the sartorial goalpost provided regular controversy all over the land.

The first problem was that the jumpers usually only provided one of the required goals. If you were lucky enough to hijack a proper football pitch that wasn't in use, it would be too big for the five-a-side games that a small group of lads could conjure up. Consequently, half a pitch was used with the proper goal at one end and jumpers at the other. An agreement would be struck to swap ends at half-time because everyone knew there was a massive disadvantage in shooting towards the jumpers. The disadvantage centred on the fact that any shot vaguely above head height would be greeted with howls of "OVER!" It was virtually impossible to score with a high shot past a short goalkeeper, as he would stick his hands up, and if the ball cleared his fingertips it would be given as over the bar. No one could prove otherwise, so, generally after some heated discussion, the goal did not stand. Meanwhile goals would be flying in for fun at the other end, with the team desperate to make their advantage count before the change of ends.

When the ball actually hit a jumper/post the interpretation fell into two distinct camps. First, there were those who argued that any 'hitting' of the jumper/post meant a goal could not stand. The second group consisted of those kids who were devout followers of the philosopher and mathematician Pythagoras. For them it was all about angles. The angle that the ball hit the jumper/post determined whether the goal should stand. Hit the inside of the pile and the ball would surely have ricocheted into the goal. If the ball passed over the middle of the assembled jumpers, it would have rebounded into play, so no goal. Of course, a stray sleeve would only serve to muddy the waters further.

The mobility of 'jumpers for goalposts' was definitely a plus point. However, it was frequently used in unscrupulous fashion by some goalkeepers. A forward could be watching the game unfolding in midfield with his back to goal. Suddenly the ball would break to him, he turns, looks up to see… the goal has moved twenty yards further away or become half its original size. Does he stop and argue the toss or attempt to score? Too late, the hesitation brings a crunching tackle and fits of laughter all around.

Hot summer days brought another problem – a complete lack of jumpers. This was usually resolved by one side playing in skins. There weren't the same worries about sunburn in those days. There were other issues though. Some players didn't want to take their tops off. The goalie had the most to lose, with increased risk of injury from a ball belted at him from close range, or multiple burns from diving on the rock hard ground. Worst of all, if someone went home you were left with only one post, and the game would have to stop until a suitable replacement was found.

The problem of using 'jumpers for goalposts' was exacerbated further when playing football in the road. In this instance the kerb or a hedge would determine one side of the goal, with the jumper being the other. You were never quite sure if a passing car would run over your jumper, so as a vehicle approached, the posts were scooped up as everyone jumped out of the way. Although traffic was an inconvenience, as the car passed, if you were in the correct position, you could fire off a crafty shot or run towards goal while the other team were still daydreaming. Think how we praise Thierry Henry for taking a quick free-kick – try risking your life to gain an advantage.

'Jumpers for goalposts' didn't just hone your football skills – it prepared you for life. It developed levels of cunning, speed of thought and a strategic thinking absent from the kids of today. If we want to win another World Cup, forget about the Russian linesman, get our youngsters out in the park or on bits of wasteland using their 'jumpers for goalposts'.

Kevin Toms

Kevin Toms and Alan Sugar. Two men at the forefront of the home computer revolution. One of them went on to become a multi-millionaire, chair a football club and have his own reality TV show. The other is all but forgotten. The time has come for us to properly honour Kevin Toms.

Kevin Toms was the creator of *Football Manager*, the original football management computer game. Kevin Toms looked a little bit like Jeremy Beadle (we know this because his cheery, bearded face adorned the cover of every edition of *Football Manager*).

Back in 1985, it didn't matter if you had a Spectrum, a Commodore, an Amstrad, an Atari or even a BBC Micro (the de facto choice of the school boffin) – you were all united by *Football Manager*. A genuine phenomenon, it was so successful that over forty different versions of the game were produced.

The game was all-consuming. Every weekend we would lock ourselves away in our respective bedrooms for hours on end. Our parents probably thought we were in there happily masturbating over pictures of Bananarama. The reality was far more exciting – we were glued to the computer screen playing *Football Manager*.

The game was delightfully simple and dangerously addictive. Like its modern-day namesake you managed every aspect of your chosen team. But matchday was the best bit, as you sat back and watched your pixelated heroes career around the pitch in a worryingly abstract fashion. Didn't they listen to anything you said in training?

Football Manager was the original game for football anoraks. For this, Kevin Toms, we salute you.

Lap of honour, the

Once upon a time, the lap of honour was reserved for champions and cup winners. It was an almost mythical event that, if you were lucky, happened once or twice a lifetime. For most fans, there was more chance of seeing a white Christmas or Halley's comet than witnessing a lap of honour.

As a player, if you'd finished mid-table, you sure as hell weren't going to celebrate the fact. You'd be down the tunnel quick-sharp and straight to the airport for two weeks in Majorca with the missus. Now, every team does a lap of honour. Every f**king season.

We want to applaud winners. Why would anyone want to applaud a team finishing fourteenth? We're not sure when this celebration of mediocrity started but we blame the parents. Or teachers.

But it is worse than that. In the old days, just the eleven players on the field at the end of the last game of the season would take part in the lap of honour. Occasionally, the manager would be goaded out of the dugout to wave the trophy in front of a terrace full of fans, but that was pretty much it.

These days, the entire first team squad of forty-odd players parade around the pitch. Not only that, they bring their kids with them. Then the office staff realise they are missing a trick and join the throng. The effect is a rag-tag band of over a hundred people circling the pitch, looking like wartime refugees in search of somewhere to stay.

It has reached the point where it would be easier for the players and officials to sit in the stands while the fans wander aimlessly around the edge of the pitch applauding in a half-hearted fashion.

Something needs to be done. FIFA need to act. Honour winners. Ridicule losers. Simple.

Leagues within leagues

Is anyone else fed up with this 'leagues within leagues' business?

It appears only Arsenal, Chelsea, Liverpool and Manchester United are allowed to compete for the title and Champions League qualification. There's a batch of clubs, with Spurs chief among them, who compete for a UEFA Cup spot. Behind them is the most tragic group, usually led by Aston Villa, who've absolutely nothing to play for apart from the honour of finishing ninth. Finally, there's the newly promoted clubs plus a Fulham or a Wigan who are destined to be involved in a relegation dogfight from day one.

Occasionally you get a surprise package, like a West Ham or a Portsmouth, who flirt with the UEFA Cup before sinking back to their natural place in the pecking order.

How we long for the days when clubs like Derby County, Nottingham Forest or even a Watford or a Wimbledon could get promotion and really worry the big boys. Until those days return, the top flight will be as dull as dishwater.

Left-wingers

We are fully aware that during the course of this book we've moaned relentlessly about the state of modern football without offering much in the way of answers. This is because we don't really have any. Our vision for football is a curious mix of 1950s middle-England and a brave new socialist utopia.

Rather naively, we envisage a green and pleasant land where football matches are played in front of capacity crowds. A land where fans stand safely together on the terraces restrained only by a picket fence and a jolly-looking policeman – a policeman, with mutton-chop sideburns, who is happy for kids to try and knock off his helmet with the roast chestnuts they've purchased for tuppence-ha'penny from a stall outside the ground.

Our pre-match entertainment would consist of a brass band bashing out a cheery rendition of William Blake's *Jerusalem*. In fact, we'd advocate replacing *God Save the Queen* with *Jerusalem* as our national anthem. If the little Englanders who attend the Last Night of the Proms can sing their hearts out to Blake's anti-industrialist canticle, then so can a bunch of overpaid footballers.

In our brave new world, most matches would finish 7-3 or 6-4. Players and fans would sink a couple of post-match pints in the supporters' club bar and then catch the No. 9 bus back to their modest homes in the suburbs. Hell, if we had our way Big Alf, our lumbering centre forward, would frequently be spotted cadging a lift to training on a passing milk float.

Of course, we're not completely stupid, we realise there's bugger all chance of this new Jerusalem coming to pass.

But football is the game of the people and, despite the creeping tentacles of commercialism, it has not yet completely lost touch with its working-class roots. Many of football's most famous sons were devout socialists. Bill Shankly's second most celebrated quote nails his political colours firmly to the mast: "The socialism I believe in is everyone working for each other, everyone having a share of the rewards. It's the way I see football, the way I see life."

Old Big 'Ead himself, Brian Clough, was another of the game's proud left-wingers. Clough was seen on the picket lines during the miners' strike and worked hard to raise funds for the miners and their families. He was also a supporter of the Anti-Nazi League.

His oft-quoted view of socialism is vintage Cloughie: "For me, socialism comes from the heart. I don't see why certain sections of the community should have the franchise on champagne and big houses." That said, we're not quite sure where publicly cuffing offenders around the ear sat with Cloughie's socialist beliefs.

There must be something about football managers and socialism. Sir Alex Ferguson, a former trade union activist, continues the socialist lineage – albeit of the watered-down New Labour variety – to this very day.

But what of the current crop of players? Can we really expect young men who are paid in excess of £40,000 a week, to beat a path to Arthur Scargill's door and demand to join his Socialist Labour Party? Probably not – yet not all modern players are devoid of a political conscience.

For a start there's Red Nev, Manchester United and England's shop steward. We know Gary got a bit militant about Rio Ferdinand's treatment by the FA but we're not entirely sure his portrayal as a bearded revolutionary is anything more than tabloid fun and games. Gary Neville aside, English football continues to suffer from a dearth of genuine left-wingers. But if we cast our net a little wider we'll discover that football can still be a hotbed of revolutionary activity. Fortunately for football, the sport that spawned Ashley Cole has also given us players like Cristiano Lucarelli, Lilian Thuram and Benny Adrion.

Cristiano Lucarelli was born and raised in a working-class neighbourhood of Livorno – a city proud of its left-wing heritage – a city that Tony Blair, if he fancies re-acquainting himself with his socialist roots, would do well to visit next time he's holidaying in Tuscany.

Lucarelli spent his childhood playing football in the streets around Livorno's docks before carving out a career in the Italian league that saw him play for Atalanta, Lecce and Torino among others.

In 2003 he joined his hometown club (then languishing in Serie B) and led them back to the top tier of Italian football for the first time in more than fifty years, scoring 29 times in the process. In 2004/05 he was the top scorer in Serie A with 24 goals in 35 matches. But Lucarelli was loved as much for his politics as his goals. At Livorno he wore No. 99 on the back of his shirt in honour of the left-wing ultras group Brigate Autonome Livornesi, who were founded in 1999. He celebrated scoring for Livorno with a dual clenched-fist salute, a gesture favoured by Communist party supporters. Lucarelli's most famous quote is a damning indictment of the modern breed of player: "Some football players pay a billion for a Ferrari or a yacht; with that money I bought myself Livorno's shirt. That's all."

Sadly, Lucarelli's relationship with his hometown club began to sour and he reluctantly agreed to join Shakhtar Donetsk for £6 million in July 2007. His return to Serie A with Parma will fuel further criticism from Livorno fans. Despite this, Cristiano Lucarelli will always be associated with left-wing ideology and, ultimately, with AS Livorno.

Lilian Thuram is, perhaps, more famous than Lucarelli. He recently overtook Michel Platini as France's most capped player and has both World Cup and European Championship winning medals to his name. In recent years, the Frenchman has also been an outspoken critic of the French political system. When, in November 2005, the current French Prime Minister, Nicolas Sarkozy (then Minister for the Interior) branded rioting youths as "racialle" or "scum". Thuram was quick to defend them, saying, "If they are scum, so am I."

In an interview in *The Observer Sport Monthly* in March 2007, Thuram again defended the inner-city kids blamed by Sarkozy for the riots that nearly tore France apart. He said, "Le Pen and his friends obviously do not know French history, or how someone like me comes to be in France, but although I am glad to be French, who can say I would not be a rioter too if I was not a footballer? I have lived like these kids. I know what the French police are like – how they try to humiliate you because of your race."

Since his initial outburst, Thuram has become something of an ambassador for French ethnic minority groups. He is now an advisor to the Haut Conseil d'Integration, a think-tank that advises the French government on race and ethnicity.

Thuram is certainly well read. He has studied the writings of Martin Luther King and Malcolm X along with Frantz Fanon, the author of *Black Skin, White Mask* and *The Wretched* of the Earth. Fanon was an activist who fought against the French in the Algerian war of independence and his work went on to inspire a generation of anti-colonial liberation movements throughout the Third World. Thuram, again in *The Observer Sport Monthly*, spoke of the link between Fanon and the Paris riots: "You can see the parallels between what Fanon is talking about and the recent violence in Paris – what people call the Parisian intifada – because it really is like the Third World out there in the suburbs." Thuram was not condoning the violence, as his political opponents suggested; he was just longing for a degree of social justice in the French political system.

Along with Patrick Vieira, Thuram tried to raise awareness of black African refugees in the country by inviting them to attend the European Championship qualifier against Italy at the Stade de France. And, while playing in Italy for Parma, Thuram confronted his own fans, who had been chanting racist abuse at AC Milan's George Weah and Ibrahim Ba. No mean feat considering the reputation of some Italian fan groups.

It would be unfair on Thuram to cast him as a left-wing activist. He has always tried to remain independent of party politics, saying "It's not a question of left or right but of trying to live together." But Lilian Thuram is prepared to stick his neck above the parapet and stand up for what he believes in. This fact alone sets him apart from so many of his contemporaries.

FC Sankt Pauli of Hamburg probably deserves an entry all of its own. If we had our way, all clubs would follow St Pauli's blueprint. Once again, to refer to St Pauli as a socialist club would be to oversimplify things. Fans are predominately left-leaning, but they are a broad church that encompasses everyone from punks and anarchists to socialists, free-thinkers and – dare we say it – regular football folk. They are probably best defined as anti-racist, anti-fascist and anti-sexist. It's not all talk either. They were the first club in Germany to ban fascist banners and chanting inside the stadium. Their Fanladen supporters' group is one of the most respected in Europe, organising an annual anti-racist tournament and helping fans overcome a wide variety of social problems, such as drug addiction, police harassment and family, school or work difficulties. The atmosphere inside FC St Pauli's Millerntor stadium is electric – and you can't really argue with a team that runs out to AC/DC's *Hell's Bells*.

But we were talking about individuals, and no one embodies the St Pauli spirit better than Benny Adrion. When Benny was released by St Pauli, he couldn't bring himself to sign for any other club. Instead, with St Pauli's backing, he set up Viva con Agua, a charity that supplies clean drinking water to children in developing countries. Adrion had been on tour to Cuba with FC St Pauli and the trip left a lasting impression on him. He returned to Cuba and helped set up facilities at various schools and nurseries that gave children access to safe drinking water. His work has also seen him embark on similar projects throughout Africa. Benny is now back in Hamburg, continuing his work with Viva con Agua; he also regularly plays for FC St Pauli's amateur, second-string side.

To us, Benny is a legend. We've not actively endorsed many things in this book but we encourage you all to visit www.vivaconagua.org

Founding an international charity is not the sort of thing that normally happens after a few days of warm-weather training in La Manga. Most top-flight players are so far up their own arses that they'd prefer to fight each other with golf clubs.

It really is time our footballers took a long hard look at themselves. The 2007 May Day Appeal For Nurses asked every Premiership player to donate a day's wages to a hardship fund for nurses. Of the 556 players asked to help only 225 contributed. Apparently, none of the Chelsea squad parted with any cash – and this for nurses who can earn as little as £19,000 a year. But it's all right, isn't it boys, you've all got private healthcare.

While we despair at the apathy demonstrated by most modern football stars, Lucarelli, Thuram and Benny Adrion give us hope. Hope that professional sportsmen can still relate to those less fortunate than themselves. Hope that, one day, the game will be awash with genuine left-wingers.

Letters to Brezhnev, Brown and Balkenende

Michel Platini is fast turning into Citizen Smith. Not content with rising to power in UEFA on a ticket of widespread reform, in September 2007 Platini decided to tackle Europe's political leaders head-on. He wrote a letter to all twenty-seven European heads of state, calling upon them to accept their role as "the last hope for a healthy and balanced future of football."

Platini stated, "A serious threat hangs over the development of European football: the malign and ever-present influence of money," before scrawling "Freedom for Tooting" at the bottom of the page in red felt pen. Possibly.

Quite what Platini was hoping to achieve with his letter, we are not entirely sure. Gordon Brown didn't seem bothered. A government spokesman came up with a typically bland response, "The Government supports the autonomy of sport and its right to self-regulation", before continuing, "We believe that football can find a way forward. The recent Premier League broadcasting deal highlights this, with money being split among the league's clubs as well as being redistributed to the grassroots…" Yes, Gordon, the money is being split, just not very fairly – which might just be St Michel's point.

Anyway, we eagerly await Platini's next move. We're sincerely hoping it involves stealing a Scorpion tank and using it to storm the Houses of Parliament.

Light aircraft

ITV's *World of Sport* didn't just introduce stock-car racing, water-skiing and wrestling to Saturday afternoons, it was also responsible for the annoying drone of light aircraft over football stadiums during the late 1970s.

The programme's title sequence featured a small plane trailing the *World of Sport* logo behind it. The idea spread like wildfire: soon light aircraft carrying messages in their wake were a regular part of the big match experience. These planes would make a dramatic, low swoop over the stadium, buzz annoyingly about for five minutes and then return to the local aerodrome. Usually, the message was mundane advertising by a local company, but occasionally a Cessna would be chartered by rival fans, so they could taunt the opposition from 1500 feet.

The boom didn't last long. By 1985, *World of Sport* had been pulled from the schedules, Dickie Davies disappeared from our screens and the light aircraft were redeployed, en masse, to the holiday beaches of the Costa del Sol.

May days

Imagine football broadcast on the telly for just one month a year? There would be riots. Satellite dishes would be torn from the sides of houses and used as natty shields, digi-boxes would be hurled at passing police vans – it would be a bloody revolution, and it wouldn't even be televised.

Not so long ago, this lack of live football was the norm. Throughout the season *Match of the Day* and *The Big Match* would screen highlights of matches on a Saturday evening and Sunday afternoon respectively. *Midweek Sports Special* would show key moments from the occasional midweek fixture but that was pretty much it.

Then, every May, something strange happened. The licence payer, starved of action for the previous eleven months, would get to overdose on live matches. It went something like this:

First came the FA Cup final, an all-day telethon that started at breakfast and continued until tea (although it was the law to have a ten-minute kickabout in the street during the half-time break, frantically acting out the drama from the first forty-five minutes).

Then, the following Wednesday, you would get the magic of the European Cup. The proper European Cup, not this Champions League nonsense. Usually there would be an English club involved and you'd cheer them like you'd cheer your own team. Close your eyes – we bet you can still see Trevor Francis stooping to head home at the back post, Peter Withe scoring for Villa or Brucie doing his jelly legs. They were crazy European nights, shared by an entire nation.

Next up, usually the following Saturday, was the annual England v Scotland fixture. We think it was supposed to alternate between Wembley and Hampden but we can only ever remember it being played in Glasgow – we must have been out shopping the year the Scots fans tore down the goalposts at Wembley. Shame, as that must've made great telly.

Then, just as you were starting to think about digging out your cricket bat from the back of the shed came another Saturday afternoon spent sat in front of the TV with the curtains drawn – this time watching the England schoolboys international. These were heady, high-pitched encounters that left you with a headache from listening to 50,000 school kids screaming at full-blast for ninety minutes.

Due to the scarcity of live football on the box, these games were the talk of the playground or the workplace the following Monday, seeping into the collective consciousness in a way that would be totally impossible these days.

And sometimes, if you were really lucky, you'd get an FA Cup final replay thrown into the mix. Usually on the Thursday night, the day after the European Cup final. Bonanza! Back-to-back nights of football.

Of course, it was the scarcity that made gorging on a month-long feast of football taste so good. Like squirrels (or maybe hamsters), we stuffed our cheeks full of live match action and lived off the memories for the next eleven months, waiting, like mayflies, for the fun to begin again (squirrels, hamsters, mayflies – what sort of analogy is this? Make your bloody mind up, eh? – *Wildlife Ed.*).

Gradually, live football on the telly took root in other months of the year. It was the beginning of the end of football as we knew it. Shame really.

Men in tights

We're far too new-age and liberal to refer to football as "a man's game," but is there really any need for players to wear gloves and tights?

As far as we can recall it was Keith Weller who first experimented with denier on the field of play. He wore a pair of white tights in an FA Cup tie against Norwich City on a freezing cold January afternoon at Filbert Street. He withstood the abuse from the terraces, even scoring in the 3-0 win.

However, it didn't catch on and it was almost a decade before anybody was brave enough to try again. That honour fell to Mirandinha at Newcastle. At a push he could be forgiven;after all, he did have the honour of being one of the first Brazilians to play for an English team. And Newcastle is bloody cold, even in summer.

Nowadays, a slight dip in temperature and it seems any kid fresh out of the academy can make his first team debut wearing tights. Don't the senior pros have any influence over these impressionable youngsters? Surely, anyone wearing tights deserves to have the piss mercilessly ripped out of them for weeks on end?

There is hope though – in the shape of global warming. Not only should we all enjoy longer, hotter summers, but the rise in temperature should spell the end of hosiery in professional football.

Men without hats

Herbert Chapman, Malcolm Allison, Bob Stokoe – proud men who liked hats. Who can forget Stokoe bounding across the Wembley turf in a Trilby? Or Malcolm Allison, doing his best Dick Tracy impersonation, in that lucky Fedora? These days, it's a baseball cap or bust.

Just as the grey squirrel (another American export) has driven our native red to the hinterlands of Britain, the American baseball cap now dominates our touchlines at the expense of more avant-garde forms of headgear. We wouldn't mind if these caps were worn at a jaunty angle or even back to front à la Kevin the Teenager. But no, they are always worn pulled tight over the manager's head obscuring his eyes. In short, the baseball cap has become a sartorial safety blanket, protecting the wearer from the relentless glare of the media.

There is hope. With Pete Doherty spearheading the revival of the pork-pie hat it can only be a matter of time before we see Arsène Wenger dancing a jig of delight around his technical area wearing nothing but a Trilby. Okay, maybe not.

Michel Platini and the French Revolution

We love Platini. We love him for being one quarter of the Carre Magique. We love him for kissing the ball before missing his penalty against Brazil in the 1986 World Cup quarter-final (on his birthday too!). We love him for supposedly bunking off training at Juventus for a crafty fag. But most of all we love him because he nailed, in one succinct sentence, what we have been trying to say for the duration of this book, "Football – It is a game before a product, a sport before a market, a show before a business." Spot on, Mickey boy.

Michel Platini might just be the man to shake up European football. His election as UEFA president caught a few people off guard, not least Lennart Johansson who, quite possibly, thought he had the job for life. Platini set his stall out early doors, rallying against the existing order by proposing to reduce the maximum number of Champions League places per country to three. Within hours of his appointment he'd turned Sir Alex Ferguson a more vivid shade of purple, with Fergie warning against any meddling with the Champions League format. Even fellow countryman Arsène Wenger was quick to round on Platini's proposals: "What people want to see is the best teams on television, to see Real Madrid against Arsenal, or Milan against Bayern Munich, that will not change." No Arsène, that's what you want. What we want is a level playing field for all teams who win – yes, win – their domestic league championship.

So will the three-times European Footballer of the Year facilitate genuine change? Here are three possible scenarios:

1. Platini, despite stiff opposition, is able to curb the influence of the G-14 (see G-Force). A salary cap of 50–60% of a club's turnover is introduced. Champions League places and television revenue are shared out fairly among all European nations. As a result, domestic leagues are more open and enjoyable, while Budapest Honvéd (hey, see I was a teenage armchair Honvéd

fan) come back from two goals down to beat Real Madrid in the 2010 Champions League final. Roman Abramovich, realising he can no longer buy trophies at will, quits Chelsea, who go bust. They reform as AFC Chelsea and begin the long climb up the non-league pyramid. Finally, Harald Schumacher is called before the newly formed Crimes Against Football Committee in Geneva and is forced to apologise for his horrific foul on Patrick Battiston in the 1982 World Cup semi-final in Seville. The French team is posthumously awarded a place in the final against Italy, and the game is replayed.

2. Platini pushes through his reforms but this results in a breakaway super league. World football is in turmoil. There are now effectively two codes: one governed by FIFA, the other, the World League Soccer (TM) owned by someone like Rupert Murdoch. It all goes a bit 'WWF wrestling' with teams like Manchester Galaxy and the Madrid All-Stars dressing in lycra and satin (think Evel Knievel circa 1976). Gradually, fans see through the charade, ditch their satellite dishes and spend their Saturday afternoons watching their local non-league club instead.

3. Platini, like all great politicians, promises much and delivers nothing. A compromise is reached and football bumbles along unchanged.

Yeah, we know the outcome. But hey, it is fun to dream.

Mike's Mini Men

'Generation Subbuteo' – that's us. There's simply no better cultural reference point to define football fans between the ages of thirty and forty-five.

We might've grown up in different parts of the country and supported different teams, but Subbuteo united us all. On those rare days when it was deemed too miserable to play outside (i.e. from October to April) we decamped to the landing or the living room to play Subbuteo.

Out of the box came the crumpled cloth and the battle was on to render the green baize smooth enough for a game to commence. This was easier said than done. Invariably the pitch would've been stuffed, absent-mindedly, back in the box. This meant crease marks that, in Subbuteo terms, were the equivalent of tectonic plates rutting up against each other. As a result, you were faced with the choice of delaying kick-off by several days and flattening the pitch with various volumes of the Encyclopedia Britannica or risking a trip to casualty by meddling with your mum's steam iron.

Then there was the carpet or table dilemma. Put it on the table and the chances were the match would have to be abandoned for tea. On highly polished surfaces, there was the added danger of the whole pitch sliding off the table and onto the floor when the action got a bit heated (always a good diversionary tactic if you were losing heavily to an older sibling). The carpet carried its own risks. First and foremost was the risk of injury, nay, tragedy befalling one of your players – carpets carried a high risk of a player being squashed under foot, which meant hours of delicate surgery carried out with a tube of superglue.

The other major problem was: the wrong type of carpet. Shagpile was de rigueur in the 1970s but made playing Subbuteo impossible. What you needed was a well-worn but flat surface of carpet or lino, anything to make the pitch run smoothly.

Unfortunately, this kind of surface was only ever found in a major thoroughfare, which further complicated matters.

Let's be clear about one thing: we loved Subbuteo. But we had issues. Scale issues. We knew there was something wrong the first time we unpacked our 'Club Edition' box. It was the ball. It was gigantic, as tall as the bloody players. Sure, it made the game playable, but it didn't half look stupid. As it turned out, this was just the tip of the iceberg.

As our Subbuteo obsession grew, we noticed other flaws. There were the freakish corner-kickers – giant players wheeled out to take corners (and this, years before David Beckham carved out a career as a deadball specialist). Even more ridiculous were the diddy guys on springs designed to take throw-ins. These amazing little fellas would either fling the ball the entire length of the pitch and off down the hall, or would snap under the weight of the oversized ball. They were utterly useless.

Then you had the trophies. We saved our pocket money for weeks to buy a stylish replica of the World Cup. It was pretty realistic, apart from the fact it was so out of scale it dwarfed absolutely everything else. In fact, lie the World Cup (Catalogue No. C182) on its side and it looked uncannily like the reclining Buddha of Bangkok, a huge golden presence looming large over the tiny, humble Subbuteo figures.

In truth, Subbuteo was as much about amassing accessories as it was about playing the game. Games themselves would usually end in bitter dispute, a hostage situation or wildcat stamping on your brother's players – it was ugly.

We craved the scoreboards, floodlights and sections of terrace that could be purchased as accessories. We would stare for hours, mesmerised by the sheer number of teams available in the official catalogue. We coveted the exotic kits from continental Europe and beyond – No. 299 Fluminense and No.502 Roma were optimistically circled in our 1981 catalogue; optimistically, because we never found a toy shop that stocked anything other than the basic teams.

At least, if you couldn't get what you wanted from the shops, you could always resort to the DIY paint job. With a bit of patience, some Airfix paint and a steady hand, you could transform the generic blue and white team, included in all standard Subbuteo sets, into something resembling Eintracht Frankfurt.

When we weren't dreaming of foreign teams, we would sit transfixed by the photograph of the 'Stadium Edition' box set in the catalogue. This was a triple-decker polystyrene behemoth that contained everything you could ever need for playing table football – hell, it probably included its own dining room table. We never knew anyone who owned this set. It was probably the exclusive preserve of posh kids who had no real desire to 'flick to kick', let alone assemble a grandstand.

These accessories didn't help you play any better. Between the two of us, we eventually amassed a grandstand and a couple of banks of terrace and all they did was impede match play. But they did add atmosphere. One Christmas, we got hold of a can of snow spray and somewhat rashly sprayed our grandstand roof and a section of the pitch white, which was okay for recreating winter football but it looked a bit stupid the following July.

eBay has given us Subbuteo freaks a new lease of life. We recently purchased a set of floodlights thinking that, with a bit of tinkering, we could turn them into avant-garde desk lamps. Unfortunately, we forgot that although described as floodlights, even in their 1970s heyday, they failed to produce enough of a glow to light even a fraction of the pitch, let alone an office. In fact, in another classic design flaw, Subbuteo floodlights appeared to be angled in such a fashion that they just shone into the middle distance, without actually illuminating anything.

Subbuteo had its rivals but none that could match its wealth of extra teams and accessories. Striker was fun in short bursts, as you frantically pressed the little players' heads to activate the bizarre kicking action, but it didn't have any longevity. And Snoccer (see Snoccer) was frankly bonkers.

Subbuteo's legacy can be seen in the numerous references to the game in popular culture. There's the obligatory Half Man Half Biscuit reference in *All I Want For Christmas Is A Dukla Prague Away Kit*. Then, there's Mike's Mini Men.

Mike's Mini Men appeared in *Roy of the Rovers* between 1976 and 1980. It featured the adventures of Mike Dailey's table soccer team, Redstone Rovers (they wore the Melchester Rovers strip, natch). *Roy of the Rovers* and Subbuteo missed a trick here, never referring to the game by its brand name in the comic strip, although clearly Mike's adventures were a four-year-long advertisment for Subbuteo. You'd think a story about a kid playing table football would be dull but you'd be wrong. This crazy guy was always losing his lucky team or having to abandon matches due to impromptu coffee mornings that were so en vogue with housewives in the late 1970s.

Even now, Subbuteo still gets its fair share of the limelight. Two excellent books have been written on the subject: Daniel Tatarsky's *Flick to Kick* is a visual feast for any fan of table soccer. Packed full of photographs, it tells the complete story of Subbuteo from its origins in the late twentieth century to the present day. Mark Adolph's book *Growing up with Subbuteo* tells the story of his father and Subbuteo's creator, Peter Adolph. A story, somewhat surprisingly, packed with fast cars and womanising that is anything but staid.

But it couldn't last forever. While kids still played proper games, Subbuteo was all-conquering but as the market for video games grew Subbuteo's popularity began to wane. In the early 1990s Waddington sold the rights to Subbuteo (along with Monopoly and Cluedo) to the American firm, Hasbro. In January 2000, Hasbro finally pulled the plug on table football, announcing that production of the game would cease immediately.

The outcry was massive, and four years later the company reintroduced Subbuteo to a new generation of kids. A quick look at the game's website shows that there are two types of Subbuteo available: 'Dream Team' and 'Urban'.

And, do you know what, it looks like they've finally cracked the problem of a bumpy pitch – two huge arches, reminiscent of Sir Norman Foster's Wembley, span the pitch, and by some architectural miracle keep the playing surface perfectly flat. In contrast Subbuteo 'Urban' is all about four-a-side street soccer, sure to feature zany pitch markings and players dressed in sleeveless tops and slip-on trainers (see What not to wear).

All this tinkering might irk the purists but Subbuteo has to do what it can to compete for the attention of the 'console generation'. With this new wave of 'Urban' players coming through and a burgeoning retro scene fuelled by the internet Subbuteo appears in rude health.

Us? We're delighted. And, to quote Half Man Half Biscuit, we're about to "send our doting mothers up the stairs with the stepladder, to get the Subbuteo out of the loft". Well, what else could we do?

Miriam's Photo Casebook

Watching football used to be difficult. Until the video recorder arrived, you either watched the match or missed it. You could watch the news for a snippet of action, or wait for the weekend football round-up on *Football Focus* or *On The Ball*. Otherwise you would never see that missed footage again.

Watching matches or highlights as they were broadcast was critical. If you didn't have two tellies you were jiggered from the outset. Partners or parents would invariably want to watch the big blockbuster film that the opposition channel would inexplicably put on at the same time as the footy highlights.

But for an entire generation of men there was one moral dilemma that outstripped all others... The year is 1978. Picture the scene: it's Saturday and you have been at work all day. You have not heard the football scores. You wade through the *Pink 'Un* and find that your team has won 6-2. You can hardly wait for *Match of the Day*. Your mood is lifted; a fish and chip supper is purchased as you head home to watch *The Six Million Dollar Man* and *The Generation Game*, waiting patiently for the football to come on.

Then, disaster. Your partner gives you the green light (yes, that green light). Your mind races, you hear the bedroom curtains shut as the theme music to the football starts. It could be a long time before your team scores six again. It could be an equally long time before you score again... What is a man to do?

Video recording, Sky Plus and the internet have made this scenario redundant. Although, if that's really the case, how come the divorce rate is still rising? We never saw this scenario in *Miriam's Photo Casebook*, but we wish we had. If only to see yet another scantily-clad lady in a footy top.

Miscellaneous Likes/Dislikes

We remember a time when getting five O-Levels was considered a major academic achievement. These days, they are given away free with packets of breakfast cereal. Why bother studying, when you can root around in a box of Frosties and pull out enough qualifications to get you into university?

Education standards are on the wane. Big time. How can we be so certain? Easy. Just ask any thirteen-year-old kid if they know what the word 'miscellaneous' means. They'll probably just shrug their shoulders and go back to blasting aliens on their portable games console.

Rewind twenty-five years and every kid knew what miscellaneous meant. At least every kid who had read *Shoot!* magazine did. Football stars of the day would be grilled, Paxman-like, in a section of the magazine called Focus On. And about halfway through the interview they were asked about their 'Miscellaneous Likes/ Dislikes.' However, before they got to tackle the thorny issue of miscellany, they had to overcome such tricky questions as:

Married: Yes, to the wife.
Car: Ford Cortina
Favourite Player: Pelé (it was always Pelé)
Best Country Visited: Spain (another easy one as before 1982, professional players were contractually obliged to holiday in Marbella).
Favourite Food: Steak.
Favourite TV Shows: The Two Ronnies, Porridge, any sports programme.

Then, just as the players were starting to relax into the interview, *Shoot!* threw them a 'Miscellaneous Likes/Dislikes' shaped curveball. We imagine that this question was met with a blank stare and a period of uncomfortable silence. Eventually the interviewer would say something like, "It's okay Ray, it just means, what sort of things do you like and what sort of things do you hate?" "Oh, okay" the slightly bemused footballer would respond.

But no matter how the question was couched, it would always elicit the same response:

Miscellaneous Likes: Golf, darts and/or snooker.
Miscellaneous Dislikes: Smoking and ignorant people.

We were left wondering who these ignorant people were? Other footballers, perhaps? We can't think who else these blokes were mixing with. After all, this was before agents and WAGs were commonplace in the beautiful game.

Anyway, after this confusion, the interview would continue as before, with such gems as:

Most Difficult Opponent: The next one.
Favourite Singers: Simply Red, Dire Straits, Luther Vandross.
Which Person In The World Would You Most Like To Meet: The person who hands me the FA Cup. Or, failing that, The Pope.

The more we think about it, the more we conclude that the bored staff writer at *Shoot!* just made it all up. But, never mind, at least we learnt something: we learnt that the word 'miscellaneous' had something to do with ignorant snooker players who liked a smoke. Armed with this level of prepubescent intelligence we're amazed we didn't get fast-tracked to Oxford or Cambridge. We'd have really enjoyed our appearance on *John Craven's Newsround* with all the other geeky child prodigies.

So, go on, ask a thirteen-year-old kid what miscellaneous means. Just don't come running to us when they gob in your face and run off with your mobile phone.

Mud on the quad

We've never set foot inside FIFA headquarters in Zurich, but to our mind it resembles a cross between Hogwarts and Magdalen College, Oxford. You know, all gothic spires and manicured college lawns, with the old boys who run world football scurrying to-and-fro across the courtyard, carrying dusty manuscripts relating to the laws of the game, and muttering things like, "oh, bother," "fiddlesticks" and "global brand expansion," under their breath.

So, when a real footballer got the job as head of UEFA, it got us thinking… Just suppose, rather than bumbling along in a bureaucratic daydream, football's governing body had to adhere to the rules of football.

Here's our plan:

All FIFA officials must wear football kit to work every day. Most of us would love that – so let's test their football credentials. The kit they wear must be a replica of a strip they have worn in their footballing heyday, anything from an old school kit to the strip of the club they played for. Wouldn't you just love to see Sepp Blatter stepping off a plane on his latest global jaunt, dressed in knee-length shorts and baggy cotton top? Or Platini, in his iconic French kit from the 1982 World Cup? We'd instigate a firm 'No Kit, No Job' policy. If you've not played football at any level, then you are out on your ear. At a stroke, the number of pen-pushers would be slashed in two.

It doesn't stop there – decision-making in FIFA is seen by football fans as a closed shop, decided by lobbying and favours. The solution is simple: when a decision is needed, it is settled on the football pitch. The twenty-four representatives on the Executive Committee have to play football to decide the outcome. That well-kept college lawn we mentioned earlier? Turn it into a five-a-side pitch – the hallowed turf where football's key decisions are reached. We'd love to see a bit of blood on the quad as the tackles fly in to determine the right to implement goal-line technology.

Placing football at the centre of all FIFA decision-making would encourage ex-players to take up the mantle. It would be interesting to see who Blatter would get onside to ensure a strong team. And how long would Jack Warner last, as he is nutmegged in a decisive vote?

Jettison the Parliamentary channel and bring us FIFA TV – debate and football – a surefire winner.

In an age where faceless bureaucrats run world football, why not give ex-players a chance to govern the game? They couldn't do any worse. Could they?

Neighbours from hell

Do kids still play football in the garden? Or are they permanently glued to their games consoles? And, if kids are staying indoors with the curtains drawn, where does that leave the neighbour from hell?

Cast your mind back thirty years – if you weren't out on a bit of scrubland having a kickabout with your mates, then you'd spend your Sunday afternoons smashing a cheap plastic football around the back garden. It was quite possible to amuse yourself for hours on end, doing keepy-ups or whacking the ball repeatedly against the garage wall.

To your average eleven-year-old this was harmless fun, but smouldering with rage, on the other side of the garden fence lurked the original 'grumpy old man'. All of us lived in fear of booting the ball over the fence and into his lair.

Actually, these old blokes weren't grumpy at all. They were full-blown fascists. Your very presence in the garden annoyed the hell out of them. You would frequently be subjected to shouts of, "Keep the effin' noise down" or "Mind my bloomin' greenhouse" (they always had a greenhouse). When you ran inside to tell your mum she would respond with something like, "Don't worry dear, that's just old Mr Potts, he's harmless enough." Harmless? The bloke was a proper little sociopath. If he found a stray ball in his garden he'd either stab it with a screwdriver or you'd be forced to watch through a hole in the fence as he put your ball on the bonfire and it turned into a bubbling, congealed lump of melted plastic.

These old-timers were pure evil. If your ball went over the fence you were resigned to losing it, unless by some miracle he was out getting his pension and his copy of the *Racing Post*. If he wasn't home, you had no option but to mount a daring rescue mission, utilising all the skills you'd picked up from watching the Iranian Embassy siege on the telly. The mission usually went like this:

If you had a sibling or mate available they would give you a leg-up over the fence before retreating to a look-out position in a bush or behind a bin. You'd then frantically search his garden for your ball – in a state of blind panic – fearful that the old git would come home and shoot you dead with his Gestapo-issue revolver. Once you'd found your ball, you'd boot it back over the fence, along with the mouldy old tennis ball you'd found festering in a flower bed. Then came the tricky part – getting back over the fence. There was no accomplice ready to give you a bunk-up. It was down to you to find a weak spot in his defences and climb back to safety. This wasn't easy, especially if your partner was frantically screaming, "He's coming, he's coming and he's got a gun!"

Fortunately, the old bastard never did catch us. But that doesn't stop us from waking up in a cold sweat, in the middle of some Vietnam-style flashback, our trouser leg snared on some barbed wire, as we desperately try to scramble back over the fence to the safety of our garden.

Perhaps today's kids are better off playing Nintendo after all.

Next goal wins

The top brass at FIFA and UEFA are constantly on the lookout for ways to improve the beautiful game. Goalkeepers are taller now, so how about making the goals bigger to compensate? Try turning a game of two halves into four quarters? Hell, anything to crack the lucrative American market.

But real change comes from the bottom up. The greatest revolutionary in football history was the first person who shouted "NEXT GOAL WINS" as a game in the local park wound down. In all likelihood, this visionary was under ten years old.

As kids, open-ended kickabouts usually petered out when the lamp-posts – annoyingly positioned to face the road and not the pitch – could no longer hold off the blackness beyond. Either that, or time would be called when the kid with the ball had to leg it home to watch his favourite TV show (for us, during the heady summer of 1983, that show was the *Happy Days* spin-off, *Joanie Loves Chachi*).

"NEXT GOAL WINS" was a classic example of that old corporate chestnut, 'blue-sky thinking'. The kid what first thunk it probably went on to head up ICI or got a seat on the board at Microsoft. How do you bring a game that is being won 37-16 to a meaningful conclusion? Easy, yell "NEXT GOAL WINS!"

Of course – and this is the real genius – the winning team would never shout it out. It was not in their interests. They had long since conquered the opposition and had spent the last half an hour strutting around like peacocks, stopping only to kneel down next to the goal and pretentiously nod the ball over the line. At this stage we're sure that in most European or South American countries, the winning team would have started to play expansive football, trying flicks and tricks as they revelled in their superiority, but in British fashion, all we can remember is trying to get as many goals as possible in order to further humiliate the opposition.

Then, just as the game is turning into a massacre, some bright spark from the losing side pipes up, "NEXT GOAL WINS" and everything changes. Weary bodies come alive. The winning team protest at the injustice of it all, but can't remonstrate too much for fear of conceding that all-important goal. Anyway, what can they do? "NEXT GOAL WINS" has been called and... it's the law.

After the shout, little kids, previously disinterested passengers in the game, would suddenly slide tackle as if their lives depended on it. Goalies, who hadn't saved a shot for about an hour, would leap like cats pouncing on their prey. There would be no let up until that final goal had been scored. Anything goes once "NEXT GOAL WINS" has been called – free-kicks were no more; for a start it was so dark you couldn't see who was tackling who. Calamitous misses would follow amazing goal-line clearances. It was the football equivalent of the Wild West, with everyone dining at the last chance saloon.

The hero of "NEXT GOAL WINS" could be anyone. It gave a chance for weaker players to gain kudos with the talented kids, which probably explains the amount of effort they put in. Just when you thought you couldn't expend any more energy, you had to. "NEXT GOAL WINS" was a matter of honour, even if you'd previously been winning by a thirty-goal margin.

Then there were the tactics of exactly when to shout the magic words. The most dangerous player on the pitch was the guy who owned the ball. Only he knew when he was likely to go home. Seasoned campaigners watched him closely as the end drew near. If he was in space near goal, you just knew he was going to shout "NEXT GOAL WINS!" It wasn't exactly sporting, but hey, it was his ball. But if the kid owning the ball was already winning he wouldn't make the call, he would leave that to the losers. The call was always made when the losing team had the ball – that was the only banker you had.

The bad feeling that "NEXT GOAL WINS" brought was unique. Everyone knew who the real winners were, but no one was interested in that once the shout had gone up. The pain of losing was always greater than the ecstasy of winning.

We watch the TV nowadays and wonder why teams play poorly for eighty minutes – we're thinking specifically the England team here – and then suddenly come to life for the final few minutes. British teams are often accused of playing sterile football and only playing positively when it is too late – this just goes to show how deeply ingrained on the national psyche "NEXT GOAL WINS" has become. If only someone could work out how to play with the passion, fervour and verve that "NEXT GOAL WINS" inspires, straight from the kick-off.

In 1993, FIFA unveiled its own version of "NEXT GOAL WINS" to the masses. It was called the 'Golden Goal'. The rule change was simple: the first team to score in extra time would instantly be declared the winner. FIFA envisaged an exciting free-for-all, as teams went hell-for-leather in an attempt to score the winning goal. It backfired. Badly. Rather than ushering in an era of attacking football, the 'Golden Goal' made teams defend with more purpose, as they became gripped by the fear of losing.

How did this happen? Well, FIFA completely missed the point. In the park or the playground "NEXT GOAL WINS" gave a team with absolutely nothing to lose a shot at redemption. If you were losing by twenty-odd goals, you could salvage some pride by scoring the final goal.

Hang on, perhaps FIFA shouldn't have abandoned the idea entirely? All it really needed were a few minor tweaks. In fact, we're convinced that in the Premiership, the use of a slightly modified golden goal could finally break the monopoly of the 'big four' (see Big four, the). Here's our idea:

At the start of each season, give every team in the league one "NEXT GOAL WINS" wildcard. They are free to use it at any point, in any game during the course of the campaign – it's entirely their call. Now this is where it gets interesting… Fulham could be getting tonked 4-0 at Old Trafford, when suddenly the ball breaks to one of their strikers unmarked in the penalty area. The manager – watching this scenario unfold in front of him – presses a big red buzzer in the dugout and "NEXT GOAL WINS" is declared. The striker scores, Fulham get the three points, and

Sir Alex goes bananas. It's three parts *It's A Knockout*, one part poker. Genius.

Sure, there are a few flaws – like 67,000 people being sent home early because some quick-thinking manager plays his joker after only three minutes. But we're sure these quirks could be ironed out. Instead, let's focus on the positives. Matches would be genuinely unpredictable and the league title would be blown wide open.

It is time for FIFA to bow to the will of the people and instigate "NEXT GOAL WINS" at the highest level. After all, a generation of school kids can't be wrong.

Nick Hornby

It is all Nick Hornby's fault.

No, not the explosion in football writing that's allowed a pair of second-rate chancers like us to net a book deal. It is bigger than that. Much bigger.

The question is this: was Hornby responsible, albeit unintentionally, for the most almighty sea-change in football history?

Think about it for a moment. Nick Hornby's *Fever Pitch* was first published in the autumn of 1992. The Premier League had just got underway and Sky Television had gambled its very future on football taking off. For Sky's punt to pay off, football needed to broaden its appeal beyond the hardcore of fans that actually attended matches.

It has always been a misnomer that football was an exclusively working-class game. For generations, the majority of fans came from working-class backgrounds, but the game also drew considerable support from the middle classes. However, until *Fever Pitch* was published, this middle-class support remained distinctly covert.

There is a wonderful passage in *Fever Pitch* that describes a young Hornby dropping his 'aitches on the terrace at Elm Park, trying to pass himself off as a genuine cock-er-nee hoodlum. Hornby was from Maidenhead, Berkshire. Nick (Davidson, not Hornby) went to school just up the road in Slough, and exactly the same thing happened there. It was as if the kids were trapped in some perpetual audition for *Eastenders*. At school – as at football – it just wasn't cool to admit you were middle class. *Fever Pitch* blew this whole charade wide open. Suddenly, it was okay to be a white-collar football fan.

Of course, the type of people who attended football didn't change overnight, but it did become acceptable to admit that you were actually an IT consultant from Stevenage or a bank manager from Solihull.

This development would've been okay in isolation, but the broadsheets and glossy Sunday supplements picked up on *Fever Pitch* and, all of a sudden, football was fashionable with the intelligentsia. People who, five years earlier, wouldn't attend a match if you'd paid them, started going to games. A mixture of constant media exposure and all-seater stadiums started to attract a totally new breed of fans. On the plus side, these nouveau-supporters challenged the media stereotype of football fans as mindless hooligans but this came at a price... an inflated ticket price. Clubs could charge a hell of a lot more for a cheap plastic seat than a spot on a crumbling terrace, especially with this new breed of fan more than willing to pay.

Slowly but surely, ordinary fans – the sort that would turn up for pointless Simod Cup games on a cold, damp Tuesday evening – were priced out of football. Atmosphere at matches is now virtually non-existent, as this new breed of fan, raised on a diet of the Premiership and Champions League, demands constant entertainment; after all, they've paid enough for the privilege.

All this is Nick Hornby's fault. If he'd not written F*ever Pitch*, middle-class fans would've happily continued attending matches incognito. Sky's great football gamble would've bombed, and the beautiful game wouldn't have turned into today's bloated, corporate monster.

Let us be clear, we think *Fever Pitch* is a work of genius, one of the best books ever written about the game we love. It certainly changed football literature for the better. Unfortunately, and unintentionally, it changed football itself. For the worse.

Nicked names

Nicknames ain't what they used to be. They are still around but, their use and originality in modern-day football has sadly diminished.

Early nicknames often referenced a player's roots. Tom Finney was known as 'The Preston Plumber', which alluded to his job. No one, before or since, has been nicknamed 'The Preston Plumber'. The nickname belongs exclusively to Finney.

Other nicknames came from the heroic feats that players performed. The best example of this is 'The Lion of Vienna', the name bestowed upon Nat Lofthouse after his two-goal heroics in England's 3-2 win over Austria in, err, Vienna.

It wasn't just heroics that earned nicknames. Eccentric acts on the pitch also brought about new monikers. Emlyn Hughes was given the nickname 'Crazy Horse' for the rugby tackle he made on the Newcastle United winger Alan Bennett. Although highly illegal and vaguely comical, fans loved Hughes' passion and attempt to stop the player by any means – in his case the nickname was entirely affectionate.

Hard men usually acquired suitably complimentary nicknames. Johnny Dexter of Danefield United was actually referred to as 'The Hard Man', although, admittedly, he was a fictional character. Ron 'Chopper' Harris and Norman 'Bites Yer Legs' Hunter were pretty self-explanatory. Andoni Goikoetxea, of Athletic Bilbao became known as 'The Butcher of Bilbao' following a tackle on Diego Maradona that broke his leg.

Sporting references are common for helping to provide a nickname. Colin Bell, the hard-running England midfielder, became known as 'Nijinsky' after the famous racehorse. Bell is one of many players to have more than one nickname – he was also referred to as 'The King of the Kippax'.

Some players have been labelled with names that, although positive, have often been something of a millstone around the neck: David Fairclough was Liverpool's saviour from the sub's bench on many occasions, most notably in the European Cup quarter-final versus Saint Etienne. He became known as 'Supersub' and the name stuck. We're sure he would've preferred to be a regular starter.

Goal poachers, the glory boys, were never short of a nickname or two. Allan Clarke was 'Sniffer', Emilio Butragueño was 'The Vulture', while the wonderfully moustachioed Gerd Müller was 'Der Bomber'. As a striker you couldn't go too far wrong with a predator-style nickname. When a player acquired such a moniker it usually stuck, regardless of a subsequent loss of form – think Francis Jeffers, still referred to as 'The Fox in the Box'.

Probably the most famous of goalkeeper nicknames was 'The Black Spider', reserved for Lev Yashin. He wore black and seemed to have loads of hands. Obvious really.

Most Brazilians use nicknames due, in part, to so many players having the same surname. For instance Ronaldo is 'Ronaldo' but 'Ronaldinho' was 'Ronaldo' before adding 'inho' to make 'Little Ronaldo'. These names often already mean something – the latest Brazilian sensation, Pato is translated as 'the duck', so the nickname is fitted as standard.

Truly great players are instantly recognisable. Do Pelé or Maradona really need a nickname? Pelé was initially dubbed 'The Black Pearl' but this was the late 1950s and political correctness had not yet gained a foothold. In reality only 'The King' or 'God' would suffice – his football ability transcended any real need for a nickname.

The greats do cause problems for their would-be successors. Think of the number of players hailed as 'The New Maradona' – Ariel Ortega, Andres D'Alessandro, Pablo Aimar, Lionel Messi – pretty much anyone coming out of Argentina under 5ft 6in.

Then there's the country-specific Maradona-u-likes: Hagi was the 'Maradona of the Carpathians', Saudi Arabia's Said Al-Owairan, scorer of that World Cup wonder-goal, was referred to as 'The Desert Maradona'. Closer to home, Sergio Torres of Wycombe Wanderers has been dubbed 'The Basingstoke Maradona'. We were never quite sure why Gazza, after his antics on the open-top bus at Luton Airport following Italia '90, wasn't christened the 'Maradona with the Big Boobies'.

Similarly Pelé spawned many named after him, most famously 'The White Pelé', or Zico, who already had a perfectly extravagant name.

With other great players, royal or military monikers usually abound. Franz Beckenbauer was 'Der Kaiser', the Emperor. Ferenc Puskás was 'The Galloping Major' and Kenny Dalglish and Kevin Keegan were both the 'King of the Kop'. Average players do not tend to have nicknames above their station.

Some players decide to bestow nicknames on themselves, the most famous of which was Paul Ince. He announced he wanted to be known as the 'Guv'nor'. Given his low status among fans (following his slightly premature wearing of a Manchester United shirt while still at West Ham), an attempt to become known as the 'Guv'nor' only heightened football fans' apathy towards him. Titles like that need to be earned. There was a general feeling that his star was not bright enough to deserve such a name. Ince was a fine player, who did not need to go in search of extra kudos; doing so really didn't help his cause. We think that David Seaman christened himself 'Safe Hands' which, if you think about it, had to be a better bet than any of the available alternatives.

Sadly, these days, the most common type of nickname is a simple derivative of a player's surname. In Britain, names need just a 'y' or an 'o' added to the end. Think: Barnesy, Clarkey, Smithy, Deano or Keano. Lazy, but common. Then we move on to Lamps, Stevie G, Becks. Different, yet somehow the same.

Very few modern players have been given nicknames that resonate. One of the best was 'The Baby Faced Assassin' for Ole Gunnar Solskjaer, a name both humorous and respectful of his skills. Since 'Gazza' we have had various incarnations of his name. Most notably the tabloids tried to saddle Wayne Rooney with the dreadful 'Wazza'. Then they tried 'Roonaldo'. Come on, let's be a bit more adventurous, eh lads? This generation of players deserve their own monikers, not variations on old nicknames.

Modern nicknames? Well, they're just rubbish.

Ol' Big Ears

It's not really a league and it's not just for champions.

At the start of the 1990s, UEFA created a monster. They christened it, without any sense of irony, the Champions League.

From 1955 to the early 1990s the European Cup was a tournament with integrity. It was a simple knockout competition that included each country's domestic champion (plus the current European Cup holder). By the early 1990s, as a sop to those threatening a breakaway European super league, UEFA began tinkering with the format. Between 1991 and 1993 they tried qualifying rounds followed by a group phase, with the two group winners going on to contest the final. The following season, semi-finals were added to the mix.

With the competition officially re-branded as the Champions League at the start of the 1992/93 season, bigger changes were inevitable. The desire for more gate and television revenue prompted the introduction of an expanded group phase, with both winners and runners-up advancing to an eight-team knockout competition.

The seismic shift came at the start of the 1997/98 season. You didn't need be volcanologist to see it coming: some countries were allowed two representatives, and thus, the Champions League was no longer the exclusive domain of league champions.

The chances of qualifying for the lucrative group stage of the competition were no longer based on merit. Instead a complicated system of UEFA coefficients was used to determine Europe's top clubs.

The new system was clearly designed to keep the G-14 (see G-Force) happy, but it has made a mockery of genuine pan-European competition. We now had a situation where teams from England, Italy or Spain could finish fourth in their domestic league and enter the qualifying rounds at the same stage as the champions of Hungary. Is it fair that the champions of a once mighty football nation, who beat England 6-3 at Wembley in November 1953 (following it up with an even more comprehensive 7-1 drubbing in Budapest a few months later), should be reduced to a bit-part role in Europe's leading cup competition?

Gone is genuine competition. In its place is a bloated, corporate monster that clogs up television schedules with a series of meaningless group fixtures. Some weeks Champions League Tuesday on ITV is like watching paint dry – not even Andy Townsend's witty pitch-side repartee can liven up another dead rubber between the likes of Chelsea and Rosenborg.

The Champions League needs to go back to basics. Strip out the laborious group stages. Return to a straight knockout competition. And make every game count. We might even get a few upsets to break the monotony of another G-14 victory.

There's little chance of this happening of course; with all his revolutionary zeal Michel Platini only had to hint at limiting participation to a maximum of three clubs from the big leagues to provoke an angry response. Meddling with the status quo just won't be tolerated.

What we really need is the big clubs to bugger off and form their own European Super League. Only then will we stand a chance of seeing a Red Star Belgrade or a Steaua Bucharest lifting Ol' Big Ears again.

Outside of the boot

Growing up in the 1970s, the ultimate in football extravagance was the shot or pass made with the outside of the foot.

By this stage in the game's development even your average park player had mastered bending the ball with the instep. But to create swerve with the outside of the foot remained an exclusively Brazilian preserve. Think Carlos Alberto's exquisite pass to Jairzinho before he crossed for Pelé to head down and force Banks into that save at Mexico '70. Think Nelinho's goal for Brazil in the 1978 World Cup third place play-off – a shot that appeared to do a reverse swerve at the end. Rivelino reproduced the outside swerve with such regularity throughout his career it appeared to be second nature to him.

In Europe, only one man had enough talent to perfect this skill. His name was Roy Race. 'Racey's Rocket' was outside-of-the-foot perfection, reproduced on a weekly basis – and with his left peg too. But, comic book heroes aside, the shot with the outside of the foot was a distinctly Latin American art form.

Then, in the 1980s, everyone was at it. Even in England. Harder to control than the inside swerve, some efforts were truly terrible. But everyone wanted to have a go. The likes of Dalglish and Hoddle could perform it at will. But then, just as quickly as the shot with the outside of the boot had arrived on these shores – it disappeared.

In modern football the stakes are so high that players rarely attempt anything as extravagant as a shot with the outside of the boot. Players are content to play the percentage game, playing safe passes and waiting patiently for a clear-cut opening. The shot or pass with the outside of the boot is just too unpredictable.

The last high-profile sighting of the phenomenon was seen in La Tournoi in 1997, when Roberto Carlos unleashed an outrageous effort that wrong-footed Fabian Barthez, nay, the entire stadium. This is how the outside of the boot swerve should be attempted – with power, to allow for that little bit of unpredictability. Carlos' shot completed the swerve cycle, if you like – the ball ending up on the same plane as it started. It was pure genius.

Of course, we wonder where the demise of this skill will lead? Kids want to 'Bend it Like Beckham' but there's no one attempting the swerve with the outside of the foot. In a generation the skill will be lost forever.

In the longer term, will our feet evolve in response to this cultural shift? If the outside of the foot is just used for balance, as a species, will we pack it all in and return to the sea? If dolphins were monkeys then, frankly, anything's possible. We await Sir David Attenborough's findings with some trepidation.

Pan-European pre-season tournaments

Dear God, do these teams not play each other enough in the Champions League or the ever-expanding UEFA Cup?

Why, at the end of every summer, do clubs take part in stupid, international, pre-season tournaments? Why do these tournaments have ridiculously over-sized trophies. Trophies that the winning captain is forced to sheepishly hold aloft as glitter rains down in the background. And why do these tournaments always seem to be played in the Ajax Arena?

What exactly is wrong with being kicked to bits in a 'friendly' match against a local non-league side?

Penalty shoot-outs

England's 4-2 shoot-out victory against Spain at Euro '96 is our nation's sole success in a competitive penalty competition. That's one pitiful victory in six attempts. Missing penalties is ingrained in the national psyche. It is not something a few days' training-ground practice prior to a World Cup is going to cure.

We propose a radical rethink:

Penalty taking should be a mainstay of the National Curriculum. Sod SATs, children as young as five should be taking penalties. In school. On a daily basis.

Scrap the morning assembly and replace it with a whole school shoot-out. They say nothing can prepare you for the high-pressure environment of taking a spot kick at a major international tournament? Well, what about being made to walk the length of the playground, with the rest of the school baying for blood, and taking a penalty?

Before we know it we'll have a generation of kids who can score penalties in their sleep. Schools will publish league tables based on their penalty strike rate. Pushy middle-class parents will move house to get their kids into the best penalty-taking establishments. To woo parents into sending their little ones private, fee-paying schools will employ former German internationals as specialist penalty consultants.

And, you never know, we might just win another penalty shoot-out.

England's shoot-out record:

World Cup 1990
4th July 1990 Stadio Delle Alpi, World Cup semi-final
England 1 West Germany 1 – Lost 3-4 on penalties
Fall guys: Stuart Pearce, Chris Waddle

Euro 96
22nd June 1996, Wembley Stadium, European
Championship quarter-final
England 0 Spain 0 – Won 4-2 on penalties

26th June 1996, Wembley Stadium, European
Championship semi-final
England 1 Germany 1 – Lost 5-6 on penalties
Fall guy: Gareth Southgate

World Cup 1998
30th June 1998, Stade Geoffroy-Guichard, World Cup
second round match
England 2 Argentina 2 – Lost 3-4 on penalties
Fall guys: Paul Ince, David Batty

Euro 2004
24th June 2004, Estadio da Luz, European Championship
   quarter-final
England 2 Portugal 2 – Lost 5-6 on penalties
Fall guys: David Beckham, Darius Vassell

World Cup 2006
1st July 2006, Gelsenkirchen, World Cup quarter-final
England 0 Portugal 0 – Lost 1-3 on penalties
Fall guys: Frank Lampard, Steven Gerrard, Jamie Carragher

Pennants

What the hell happened to football pennants? During the 1970s and '80s they were absolutely everywhere.

First and foremost, they would be exchanged by the two captains prior to kick-off in European competitions or international fixtures. We remember this clearly because the handover was always captured on film and reproduced in the newspapers, magazines and comics of the day. This never happened in domestic football, aside from, perhaps, League and FA Cup finals.

From this, we conclude that in the 1970s, the exchange of pennants represented the pinnacle of international diplomacy. Perhaps it was the humble pennant exchange that prevented nuclear apocalypse as, aside from the reciprocal transfer of spies during the cold war, the pennant swap was – pretty much – the only genuine cultural exchange between East and West.

Pennants weren't just exchanged and forgotten about. Oh no. They would be proudly displayed in the boardroom or in the manager's office. How did we know? Because they were there, pinned to the wall, and clearly visible on camera in every interview *Football Focus* ever did. This level of media exposure (these days, the exclusive realm of the Beckhams) made pennants very desirable for young football fans growing up in the 1970s. Every boy's bedroom had at least one. We're not sure what the attraction was. They were just triangles of satin or plastic. Sure, they often had a luxurious material trim but they didn't serve any actual purpose. Yet they appealed to the collector in all of us.

Shoot! and *Roy of the Rovers* would carry half-page adverts offering a dazzling array of international pennants. Owning a Borussia Mönchengladbach pennant appealed to our obscurist nature (see I Was A Teenage Armchair Honved Fan), and really sorted the men from the boys. Unfortunately, our collections were hindered by the economics of the day. The 1970s were turbulent times and, living in the shadow of stagflation, we had better things to spend our money on than football pennants. After all, forty-five pence was an awful lot of money in 1978.

Sadly, pennants have all but vanished from the modern game. Occasionally a misguided captain (usually from an emerging European nation) will bring one along to the pre-match coin toss, but all this does is create an awkward silence, with the opposition captain having nothing to offer in return.

There is hope, however. Visit any non-league clubhouse in Britain and the walls are sure to be decorated with a smattering of pennants, none of them more recent than 1985, and all of them covered in a good half-inch of dust.

Pennants – you were useless, but we don't half miss you.

Perfect pitch

Britain has changed. We have it too easy. Kids don't have to struggle to get new kit, boots or decent pitches to play on. The academies have opened up a perfect world for our children to go into, and this is what all parents strive for. Think again, soccer mom.

Drive past open expanses of ground on any day and no one is playing football. A few kids are skateboarding; a few are comparing phones or the latest handheld gadget. You might occasionally see a dad kicking a ball around with a toddler but there aren't any 'jumpers for goalposts' (see Jumpers for goalposts) in the modern world. Cut to Brazil. Beaches, streets and parks are awash with children and adults of all ages playing football. They don't need the latest kit. They don't need perfect conditions. They just need a ball.

One of this book's co-authors, Shaun Hunt, grew up playing football in rural Cornwall, where the cows roamed free. There were natural hazards for budding footballers. The hard coating of a cow turd hid a chocolate mousse interior, ripe for a slide tackle. No one shirked a challenge near the obstacle. So what if your T-shirt was covered in shit; honour was at stake. In wet weather the only footwear allowed was a welly. Football in wellies? How did that work? Well, for a start, you couldn't welly it, because that would mean your boot would fly off and become entangled in the nearest gorse bush. The game wouldn't stop while you fished it out, either. Water soaked through your cagoule and your feet froze but you played on regardless of the conditions.

The desire to play football in all weathers should be the starting point for all kids. Not the desire to play on a perfect pitch in a perfect kit, with a perfect ball. Bring back park football, street football – and football dreams.

Peter Barnes Football Trainer, the

Back in the 1970s, the game wasn't awash with money like nowadays. Players had to explore every available avenue to earn a crust. While football's biggest stars landed advertising deals with leading brands, the games lesser-known names had to think laterally. And that usually meant endorsing products that were, quite frankly, bonkers.

Franz Thijssen might've had indestructible balls (see, err, Franz Thijssen's indestructible balls) but Peter Barnes had a football on a string. Yes, the imaginatively named Peter Barnes Football Trainer was nothing more than a football on a string. Like we said, bonkers.

According to Peter it was a "fantastic way to develop your football skills and ball control." To us, it looked like an accident waiting to happen. One end of the rope was attached to the ball while the other end clipped to your waist. Like an extra-long umbilical cord, you were permanently connected to the football. But why? Surely, after a couple of keepy-ups you ended up on the floor in a tangled mess of legs and rope?

The only conceivable benefit was the ability to welly the ball as hard as humanly possible, and never have to run more than five yards to retrieve it. But even that simple manoeuvre must've carried a high risk of the ball pinging back and whacking you in the goolies?

We really hope Peter Barnes made some money out of the franchise but we can't recall anyone who actually owned one. We're guessing the Peter Barnes Football Trainer went the same way as those other great inventions of the decade. Somewhere, just off the North Circular, there's a huge lock-up, packed to the rafters with Betamax video recorders, sandwich toasters, and footballs on bits of string.

Played by males

What is it about blokes? We are really just geeks obsessed with meaningless statistics. Football statto? Trainspotter? Computer nerd? Same anorak, different colour.

Maybe this obsessive behaviour adds purpose to our meaningless lives. After all, women do pretty much everything better, faster and with a lot less fuss. All we can do is huddle together at the end of the platform or sit hunched in front of an Excel spreadsheet committing a series of facts and figures to memory… it's our destiny as a gender.

The football fan is especially susceptible to this sort of character defect. Football is all about statistics. We all know somebody who can recite the score, scorers and attendance from every FA Cup final since records began.

The emergence of fantasy football and computer simulations has taken this obsession with statistics to new heights. But today's fantasy football was preceded by a different type of fancy: play-by-mail. And this was hardcore.

In the 1980s, if you scanned the back pages of any football magazine you would find advertisements for play-by-mail, each claiming to be an authentic recreation of the beautiful game.

The game involved choosing teams and playing a match or series of matches in turn. You'd make your selections and post them to a dead letter box somewhere in Essex. A computer would then generate results for your team and send them back to you, all via Royal Mail. It was like waiting for your A-level results, only worse. And it happened every week. Come to think of it, in those far-off days before eBay, it was probably just our play-by-mail traffic that kept the Post Office afloat.

You could even make up your own player names. This was the cause of much teenage hilarity as Dick Fruit won back-to-back golden boot awards. Hell, we were even trailblazers for exotic foreign imports. At some point in the spring of 1985, Brazilian playmaker and erstwhile lothario, Phoenix Emeraldo, arrived in

England and shook the play-by-mail world to its very core.

The internet has all but replaced play-by-mail. But, in simpler times, a nerdy bloke with a love of statistics spent his entire life churning out fictitious results onto original computer paper – you know, that stuff with the faint green lines, holes down the side and the perforations. He'd then post it back and charge you £1.25 for the privilege. You never quite knew whether the results you achieved were due to some superb strategic insight or just the random machinations of the host computer. Even when the stats finally arrived in the post, it would take forever to find your result among the myriad of useless information, but that only heightened the experience.

Of course money played an enormous part in determining success. Play-by-mail had the same problem with big investors as modern-day football. The inequalities in wealth were staggering. In reality, our pocket money was no match for some geeky middle-aged accountant, living alone in a flat in Crouch End. Try as you might, on a shoestring budget, you could not oust the big spenders, something Shaun found out to his cost. Long before Steve Gritt and Alan Curbishley embarked on co-management, Shaun and a mate from school co-owned Queen of the South in a play-by-mail game. With their combined resources they moved swiftly through the divisions, laughing as they swept aside tactically inept managers and computer-generated teams with the combined might of £3.75 a week. But it was unsustainable, funds were short, diversions were many. It didn't help that in order to make the weekly postal deadline, they had to meet in the bus park at secondary school before lessons started. Shaun and his mate had a matter of minutes to review the results and sort out a strategy for the following week. Then they had to give the envelope to the school bus driver (who doubled as the village milkman) who, in turn, delivered it to Shaun's mum to post. Really, you couldn't make it up.

Technology moves on, dragging nerdy blokes in its wake. Fantasy football and computer games have long since replaced play-by-mail. Sometimes we pine for simpler times – times when a computer nerd in Romford could make or break your week.

Power in a union

There is one union Thatcher failed to nobble. Forged early in the twentieth century, its members would regularly convene above a pub on a cobbled Lancashire back street.

According to legend, the chairman of this shadowy organisation wears a golden glove. It is widely believed that the glove holds mystical powers and was commissioned in direct response to the golden boot awarded to the striker who breaches union picket lines the most times in a single season.

You may think that it's Sepp Blatter who makes the rules, but take a look at any major law changes and you will see the Union at work.

It wasn't all that long ago that goalkeepers were being barged into the net in FA Cup finals. These days, goalkeepers are better protected than your average world leader. Those blokes in the orange tabards with the walkie-talkies? They're not matchday stewards – you fools – they're MI5 operatives. You can't point a finger in the direction of a keeper at corners without the referee blowing. A keeper goes down 'injured' and the game is stopped immediately. Where's the fun in that? Watching defenders diving to save the ball while the keeper lies prostrate on the turf was good, old-fashioned entertainment.

Then there's substitutions. It took eighty years for a single substitute to be introduced to the domestic game. The move from one to three subs took just twenty-five years. Hmmm. The single substitute was invariably an outfield player; goalkeepers didn't stand a chance. The move to three substitutes meant that a goalkeeper and two outfield players could be named on the bench. The British chapter of the Union can't take the full glory for this rule change – it was their comrades on the continent who pioneered the cause. And, as early as 1982, Aston Villa's Nigel Spink took full advantage of this loophole, replacing Jimmy Rimmer after only ten minutes of the European Cup final, and going on to produce a match-winning performance.

With replays scrapped, penalties are now the only way to decide one-off matches. Who in football would welcome more penalty shoot-outs aside from the Germans? Yep, you've guessed it... goalkeepers. With penalties the keeper can't lose. If they don't save any, everyone says the taker is supposed to score from twelve yards. If they save the penalty, no matter how poorly taken, they are heroes.

Even if the penalty fails to hit the target, it is put down to the goalkeeper's antics on the line. Have you noticed how referees seem powerless to prevent keepers advancing off the line to save the ball before the penalty has been struck? This has got to be the most abused law in football. How many times are penalty kicks retaken? Hardly ever. The Union has the match officials in its pocket. Even the stutter in the penalty-takers' run-up has been banned to make it easier for the keeper.

The Goalkeepers' Union has successfully implemented widespread reform: pushing through greater protection for their members, extra spaces on the bench, and championing the penalty shoot-out so that their members can assume starring roles. And they say trade unions are toothless, just relics of a bygone age?

You want proof of the Goalkeepers' Union in action? Just watch what happens at the end of a match when one of the two keepers has played badly or let in a hatful of goals. There's always a warm embrace, a shrug of the shoulders, and a genial chat about the game. This can't be coincidence.

Who are the leaders of this powerful interest group? No one knows for certain, but one particular name keeps cropping up with alarming regularity. He was the perpetrator of the worst foul in World Cup history – a tackle that didn't warrant a booking, even though the recipient left the field on a stretcher, minus teeth. No outfield player would have got away with a crime like that. In today's game such a tackle would incur a lifetime ban and a custodial sentence. Harald Schumacher got away free. Could his be the 'invisible hands' controlling this mysterious organisation? Just think about it.

Prawn sandwiches

To the untrained eye Roy Keane is a madman. Not only that, he's a madman with a dog. A big scary dog.

Over the years, we've worked for some pretty crap bosses, and have penned (though never posted) some pretty forthright resignation letters – but Roy actually went and did it. Slap bang in the middle of the World Cup to boot. "You're a f**king wanker and you can stick your World Cup up your arse. The only reason I have any dealings with you is that somehow you are the manager of my country. You can stick it up your bollocks." Which, all told, leaves us with the disturbing mental image of Mick McCarthy attempting the unique feat of simultaneously shoving the World Cup up both his arse and his bollocks. Nice.

As is often noted, the line between genius and madness is perilously thin, and despite his bolshy strops, when musing on the changing nature of football fans, Roy Keane hit the nail on the head. That his 'prawn sandwich' outburst occurred as long ago as 2000 makes him something of a prophet. So much so, it's worth recounting the shaven-headed soothsayer's tirade in full: "Sometimes you wonder, do they understand the game of football? We're 1-0 up, then there are one or two stray passes and they're getting on players' backs. It's just not on. At the end of the day they need to get behind the team. Away from home our fans are fantastic, I'd call them the hardcore fans. But at home they have a few drinks and probably the prawn sandwiches, and they don't realise what's going on out on the pitch. I don't think some of the people who come to Old Trafford can spell 'football', never mind understand it." Roy, we agree one hundred per cent. And not just because we're scared of dogs.

It's all too easy to criticise Manchester United fans. It is true that the atmosphere at Old Trafford can be strangely muted with the visiting supporters providing the noise and the colour but, as Roy points out, away from home the Manchester United fans are superb.

It's not that the fans don't want to sing, it's just that at Old Trafford they are either priced out of the stadium or their influence is diluted by the hordes of day-trippers and corporate freeloaders who just want a nice day out.

It's not just Manchester United: most of the big clubs are similarly afflicted. An afternoon at Ashburton Grove (the Emirates, if you must) makes the old Highbury Library look like a rave venue. The entire middle tier (it's probably called the Dress Circle) empties dead on half-time as the corporate luvvies retreat indoors to enjoy their canapés and champagne. It's sickening – make the bastards survive on a cup of Bovril and an out-of-date Wagon Wheel.

Roy was almost right when he said that the prawn sandwich brigade "don't realise what is going on out on the pitch." He just needed to substitute the word 'realise' with 'care'. Following a club through thick and thin isn't on the agenda. The investment isn't emotional. It's financial. Just another opportunity to schmooze and be schmoozed. If that's how you want to spend your afternoons, please f**k off back to Twickers.

Football is about passion and commitment. It's not about accepting free tickets to the FA Cup final, but only if you can squeeze it in between Ascot, Henley, Wimbledon and sodding Cowes week. It is time to reclaim the game. We don't advocate hooliganism, but then again, we don't see much wrong in running amok in the corporate lounge, upturning a few hostess trolleys. To paraphrase our Roy, "You can stick your prawn sandwiches up your f**king bollocks!"

Premiership anthem, the

Did we miss something? Has the Premiership declared itself a sovereign state? An official anthem? Do behave.

As if the pre-match build-up wasn't preposterous enough already, we now have the absurd spectacle of the two teams standing to attention in front of the motley selection of directors box dignitaries, while what sounds suspiciously like a Premiership anthem plays in the background. Even Kim Jong-il would consider it a touch over-orchestrated.

They've invented their own sodding anthem. What next? Are they going to start inter-marrying? Bumping off undesirable family members? Ah yes, they already do that. It's called relegation.

Racey chat

Did anyone else find the Cadbury's Caramel bunny arousing? We hope so, or we need therapy. In much the same way that cartoon rabbits should not be sexy, neither should cartoon ladies in football comics. But in adolescence, it wasn't the great storylines or the lure of free gifts that kept us avidly reading *Roy of the Rovers* – it was Penny Race. She was a MILF long before anyone had coined the term. And, as the wife of Roy, she was quite possibly the original WAG.

Think of a slightly more buxom Victoria Principal (you know, Pam Ewing in *Dallas*). She would pop up regularly in a pencil skirt, blouse, high heels and stockings. And damn, was she pretty. As adolescent fantasy figures went, she was right up there with Daisy Duke. How we craved something slightly risqué – an upskirt shot of Penny, or a sketch of her in a skimpy towel answering the door – you know, something that would turn Blackie Gray's hair, well, grey.

Then, in the issue dated 15th September 1984 (we know, we kept it), all our prayers were answered. Penny was pictured in a tight-fitting referee's costume celebrating Roy's thirtieth birthday. Lucky Roy. When we turned thirty, nothing like that happened to us. And this was the same day that Roy was granted the Freedom of Melchester. Some blokes have all the luck, eh?

Back then it was hard to talk about. There was no way we were going to mention to our mates the strange stirring in our loins that Penny generated. With the benefit of hindsight, we know it is perfectly normal to fantasise over cartoon women. After all, who doesn't fancy the cartoon pants off Mrs Incredible? But, in those days, there was an innocence about our feelings for Penny Race. She didn't work at being a sex symbol, it just happened. She was a natural beauty, needlessly killed off in the later, sensationalist years of *Roy of the Rovers*.

Rest in Peace Penny Race. You were the original MILF, WAG and cartoon sex symbol. And dear God, we fancied you.

Rattles, milk crates and rosettes

Any archive footage of football crowds before 1960 is required, by law, to include the following: someone holding a rattle; a kid carrying or standing on a milk crate; and impossibly cheery men wearing rosettes in club colours.

Imagine the upset rattles would cause if they were re-introduced these days. The European courts would be inundated with personal space issues. The accident claim companies would be lining up outside grounds offering 'no win, no fee' schemes if tinnitus could be proven. Similarly, milk crates would be confiscated at the turnstiles by stewards, never to be seen again, as health and safety officials waged war. Forget about milkmen surviving in the supermarket age, how did they cope with kids nicking their crates every Saturday morning?

And then there's grown men wearing what can be only be described as a male corsage. We remember them being most prevalent on FA Cup final day. But with so many supporters packed onto the terraces, how did the rosette survive from one game to the next?

Time and tide waits for no man. Scarves and polyester shirts have replaced the humble rosette as a show of support. Rattles, milk crates and rosettes RIP. The modern world has disowned you all.

Replica shirts

£39.99 for a flimsy polyester shirt? Ah yes, but this new ultra-light, dry-weave, microfibre mesh actually wicks moisture away from your body, increasing breathability and improving performance.

Don't shirt manufacturers get it? Replica shirts are not for elite athletes. They're for young kids. And fat blokes who like a beer. Surely Nike would be better off spending millions of pounds researching a shirt that can repel curry stains, or that can clean itself simply by being left at the bottom of the wardrobe for a couple of weeks? Now, that would be progress.

As for the price, you can buy a replica shirt from Thailand on eBay for about a tenner. The quality looks pretty good and in all probability they come from the same factory as the official shirts retailing at £40. How can sportswear companies continue to justify the hefty price tag? In 2003, ten companies including Manchester United, The FA, Umbro and JJB Sports were fined by the Office of Fair Trading for colluding to keep the price of replica shirts artificially high. Five years on, have any of you noticed any significant reduction in price?

Robbie Williams

Robbie Williams has his knockers. But we love him.

When the tabloids reported that Our Bob was spending millions on an indoor soccerdome, so that he and his showbiz pals could have a kickabout, they seemed to imply that he was being a touch extravagant. We think it is a bloody great idea. If we had that sort of cash there'd be an indoor soccerdome at the bottom of both of our gardens, and we'd be playing football 24/7.

This sort of behaviour is nothing new. Rod Stewart started the craze for full-size football pitches, installing one in the grounds of his Essex mansion. Anyway, who could possibly begrudge Robbie inviting Elton, Rod and Becks round for a game of celebrity headers and volleys?

But Robbie is not content with kicking around with his showbiz pals in the back garden. He's gone one step further. He's set up his own football team, LA Vale. Robbie and his mates play their football in the grandly named Los Angeles Premier League, and they are doing rather well. That they were undefeated in their first sixteen matches won't be a surprise to anyone who has watched Robbie play in televised celebrity matches – the lad's a bit handy.

We can't help admire Robbie's passion and dedication to the beautiful game. With so much money, and so many temptations, the pressure not to self-combust must be enormous. Football certainly has a great capacity to keep people grounded.

Hopefully, football will keep Robbie out of mischief. After all, an afternoon of dressing room banter is worth a thousand sessions with a Hollywood shrink. It's a damn sight cheaper too.

All of a sudden that extravagant soccerdome doesn't seem like such a bad investment. Good on you, Robbie. If we make it to LA promoting this book, we'll bring our boots. We'd love a run-out.

Roberto Dinamite

Brazil is not a nation that suffers from a dearth of forward options. The names of Pelé, Rivelino, Zico, Romario, Ronaldo and Ronaldinho trip off the tongue before the brain has properly engaged.

Ask most people who the greatest Brazilian striker of all time is and you'll get the same answer: Pelé. Ask us the same question. Go on, we know you want to.

Sure, Pelé was good but, ever since the 1978 World Cup in Argentina, we've only had eyes for one Brazilian. He was dynamite. Roberto Dinamite.

We knew that Carlos Roberto de Oliveira, or Roberto Dinamite for short, wasn't the greatest striker Brazil had ever produced, but he had the best name. We were just kids, but for the duration of the summer of '78, playgrounds were full of boys screaming "Dynamighteeey," whenever they scored past the disinterested, nerdy kid in goal.

Dinamite wasn't a bad player either. His official website has him down as scoring 708 career goals for Vasco da Gama, and 26 goals for the Brazilian national side. Three of those international goals came during the 1978 World Cup. Roberto scored the only goal in Brazil's 1-0 victory over Austria in the first group stage, and he netted twice in the 3-1 win against Poland in the second group stage.

Roberto Dinamite also made it into Telé Santana's 1982 World Cup squad – a squad widely regarded as the second greatest side in Brazilian history, behind the legends of Mexico '70. Although, unsurprisingly he couldn't force his way into a side containing; Socrates, Zico, Eder, Falcao and, err, Serginho.

To be honest, we'd all but forgotten about Roberto Dinamite. That is, until the summer of 2002, when you couldn't turn on a radio without "Miss Dynamite-tee-hee" blasting out at full volume.

You see, when Roberto Dinamite retired from the beautiful

game, he didn't sit around trading on his former glories. Oh no. First came the perky R&B phenomenon, Ms Dynamite, who not only did a neat line in radio friendly hip-hop, but also scooped the 2002 Mercury Music Prize for her debut album, *A Little Deeper*. Then, in 2004, came the release of the movie *Napoleon Dynamite*, a film – we can only assume – that is about another of Roberto's media-savvy offspring*. So, let's hear it for Roberto Dinamite. He might not have been the greatest striker ever to appear for the Seleção, but he sure had one hell of a name. Not only that, he fathered an entire 'Dinamite Dynasty'. Possibly.

*Oh, okay, he didn't really have anything to do with Ms Dynamite or Napoleon but we can dream, can't we? Actually, Roberto Dinamite's post-football career has been anything but boring. Rather than run a bar, or do TV work, Roberto has pursued a career in politics. He is a member of the Brazilian Democratic Movement Party (PMDB) – who, according to the internet, are a curious alliance of liberals and members of the former guerrilla movement MR-8. He has also been a Deputy in the state assembly of Río de Janeiro since 1994. So there.

Robson Gold

Who's bright idea was it to let Bryan Robson endorse shinpads? A more unlikely marriage of player and product we can't imagine.

Close your eyes and think of Bryan Robson. We guarantee you are seeing him being led from the pitch, clutching his injured shoulder, at the 1986 World Cup in Mexico. This wasn't an isolated incident. Captain Marvel was always injured.

Robson broke his left leg twice and his right ankle once, while still at West Bromwich Albion. At Manchester United he was hugely successful, but he still suffered horrendous bad luck with injuries. There probably isn't a bone in his body that hasn't been broken.

With this in mind, it seems incredible that Robson Gold shinpads ever went into production. But they did. And they sold by the bucket load. As kids, we were grateful to stick cheap plastic shinpads down our socks. Pads with a foam backing that caused your shin to sweat at an alarming rate, forcing you to peel them off your leg at the end of the game. However, we counted ourselves lucky. A few years earlier the only option was to stuff back issues of *Battle* comic down your socks and hope for the best.

Robson Gold changed shinpads forever. Robson's pads included revolutionary ankle protectors, industrial-strength plastic, and a Velcro strap that held them firmly in place on your leg. They made you feel like Robocop. Best of all they had Bryan Robson's signature monographed, on the front, in gold. Robson Gold. Geddit?

Thanks to Robbo we never suffered broken shins. Dislocated shoulders were another matter entirely.

Rock DJ

The job of a stadium announcer used to be simple: read out the teams, the half-time scores and the attendance. There was the occasional bonus of a car that had to be moved or a husband called away to the birth of his child, but that was pretty much it.

These days, being in charge of the stadium PA system is akin to presenting the breakfast show on Radio One. The job is no longer one of conveying information – it's now all about managing the matchday experience.

Remember a time when rival sets of fans would trade chants in the build-up to kick-off? The singing would increase in volume and ferocity as 3pm approached, so as the teams came out the atmosphere would be at fever pitch. Nowadays, you get the idiot with the microphone demanding that you, "make some noise" or even worse, "give it up" for team X or team Y. Give what up exactly? The will to live?

What this new breed of DJ fails to understand is, we can't be bothered to make any effing noise. This is because the cretin has just spent the last fifteen minutes playing a curious mega-mix of handbag house and Wagner's *Ride of the Valkyries* over the tannoy, in a pathetic attempt to generate some excitement. It's not rocket science – turn the PA off, and let the fans make the noise.

Not content with ruining the pre-match atmosphere, it is now compulsory to pump music through the PA every time the home team scores a goal. They might be mates with Lucas Radebe, but we don't want to celebrate every bloody goal with the Kaiser Chiefs.

At least with goal celebrations DJs attempt to keep abreast of the hit parade. Win a trophy and it is forever 1985. League or cup celebrations are always drowned out by Queen's *We are the Champions*. Then comes *Simply the Best* by Tina Turner. Inexplicably, Status Quo's *Rockin' All Over The World* completes the soft rock triumvirate. Worse still, supporters actually sing along to this garbage. Okay, Chelsea fans, you might have won the league for the first time since 1955 but, dear God, we really didn't, "li-li-li-like it, li-li-li-like it" when you sang along to the Quo like an embarrassing uncle at a wedding.

Of course, like hospital radio, the matchday DJ has the ability to inflict their music tastes on a captive audience. This can have a profound effect on your average football fan. In the early 1990s, Nick swears he heard *Black Velvet* by Alannah Miles three seasons running at Swindon Town's County Ground. Nearly twenty years on, he can't get any closer than Junction 16 on the M4 without breaking into a rakishly out-of-tune rendition of the song. His family are encouraging him to seek professional help.

As a rule of thumb, music at matches should be limited to the half-time interval. And the wannabe DJs should stick to weddings, parties, anything but football.

Rock Me Amadeus

"Amadeus, Amadeus. Oh-oh-oh, Amadeus."

We remember being easily scared and confused as kids. Nick would always turn his trainers upside down and shake them vigorously before putting them on, a result of watching a TV documentary about scorpions hiding in shoes in the Australian outback, particularly stupid as Nick lived near Slough. While Shaun got nervous around mirrors, fearing he might accidentally break one and heap seven years of bad luck upon his idol, Kenny Dalglish. Our young minds were still developing and sometimes we got in a muddle.

So imagine our confusion, when in 1985 someone called Falco released a song called *Rock Me Amadeus*. To us, Mark Falco was a striker with Tottenham Hotspur. On first listen, it seemed remarkable that he could sing in both English and German. But it was just about possible – Falco wasn't always in the Spurs first team; perhaps on his days off he had taken German lessons?

Then we saw the video. Man, that was really confusing. Was that really Falco in the dinner jacket? Or was he the scary bloke in the wig? And where was Garth Crooks as the debauchery unfolded on screen?

Of course, with the benefit of a half-decent secondary education, we found out that it was possible for two different people to share the same name. Which is just as well, as Ronaldo simultaneously playing for Manchester United and Real Madrid would've really messed with our minds.

Rotation, rotation, rotation

Rotation is all very well for certain things: crops, planets or old skool vinyl. Rotation is not okay when it comes to football teams.

Here's a thing: why don't managers field their strongest team for every match? They might just win a few more games. It certainly used to work like that. When Liverpool won the league title in 1965/66 they used just fourteen players – all season. That's the same number a manager is permitted to use in a single match these days.

Yes, super-sized squads mean managers have to juggle players and massage egos, but there must be something to be said for a small tight-knit squad, where every player knows his job, and his place in the pecking order.

Perhaps it's the players' fault. They seem so fragile nowadays (and not just in the ego department). They're always bloody injured. Hardly any players are ever-present over the course of a season any more. Think back thirty years, and you could guarantee your club would have three or four stalwarts who would go a whole season without missing a game. Phil Neal played 365 consecutive matches for Liverpool between 1975 and 1983 – that's eight years without missing a competitive fixture.

The tinkermen will blame the increased pressure on players due to the sheer volume of matches. They will insist that players need to be rested to prevent burnout. They will also claim that different competitions require different personnel. It's all bollocks. Put out your strongest team – all the time. You'll win more matches. Guaranteed.

Safe standing

Throughout this book we've criticised modern football. For the most part we've been flippant and, it's fair to say, a touch pious. There is, however, one topic we'd like to play with a completely straight bat. That is the issue of safe standing at football matches.

We're prepared to cast aside the cheap shots and rubbish jokes for a few paragraphs because any discussion of safe standing at football matches will always be linked with the Hillsborough disaster.

To this day, the events of 15th April 1989 haunt all football fans. Ninety-six Liverpool supporters lost their lives attending a football match. Even after all these years, just typing those words sends a shiver down our spines – God only knows how the family and friends of those who lost their lives at Hillsborough feel. That ninety-six people lost their lives following the team that they loved is a tragedy that could and should have been averted.

The cover-up that followed Hillsborough is nothing short of a disgrace. In the hours that followed the disaster, the blame was laid firmly at the door of Liverpool supporters. In the days that followed, British journalism hit an all-time low. A well-known tabloid paper published an article entitled 'The Truth' that claimed that Liverpool fans had robbed and urinated on the dead, and had fought with the police. The paper's version of events couldn't have been further from the truth and was contradicted by television footage of the event which showed anguished fans assisting the emergency services, carrying the injured to safety on stretchers made from advertising hoardings.

The inquiry into the tragedy, led by Lord Justice Taylor, concluded that the main cause of the disaster was "the breakdown of police control." Hillsborough was certainly the result of sheer incompetence on a massive scale.

Despite the attempted cover-up and the media lies, all real

football fans know that Liverpool supporters were the innocent victims of a terrible tragedy. What makes Hillsborough so poignant for all fans is that it was a classic case of 'there but for the grace of God...' It really could have been any of us. We'd all witnessed the overcrowding, the poor policing and the non-existent stewarding. We'd all watched football from inside those barbaric cages. We knew it could've been us.

You might think it strange that fans, who for years stood in appalling conditions, would champion the return of terracing, but there is an important distinction. We don't want to simply turn back the clock. We want to stand, but on modern, properly regulated, safe terracing. It's not just us: a recent survey of 2,000 football fans shows that ninety per cent favour the return of standing areas. Mike Hancock, the Lib Dem MP for Portsmouth South even tabled an early day motion asking for a debate on the issue. However, the then Sports Minister, Richard Caborn, like his predecessors, was not for turning.

The abolition of terracing in top-flight football has, more than anything else, destroyed the atmosphere at English football grounds. Take away the terracing, and you take away the ability for fans to move freely about. Thus those who want to sing can't congregate together. Instead, they are scattered to the four corners of the stadium. Even sitting near friends requires a great deal of forethought and planning. Then there is the issue of people who won't sit down in their seats. Surely, this causes more danger than standing on a designated terrace. These days, no game is complete without frequent shouts of "sit daaarn" from irate fans, who object to people standing up in front of them.

Safe standing at top-flight matches is not without precedent. In the Bundesliga, standing at matches never went away. Not that stadium development has stood still. Quite the opposite. Many of the grounds modernised for the 2006 World Cup include large areas of removable seating that can be converted to safe terracing for Bundesliga games, and then back to seats for Champions League, UEFA or international football. The most famous example is the Westfalenstadion, home of

Borussia Dortmund. This ultra-modern stadium can hold 81,264 with a combination of seating and terracing or 67,000 seated spectators. The atmosphere it generates for league games is intense, so much so that the ground is nicknamed 'The Opera House of German Football'. The massive Südtribüne can hold 27,000 standing supporters. Converting the Westfalenstadion stadium from terracing to all-seater takes just two days. So there is no problem playing a midweek European tie, followed by a Bundesliga game on a Saturday.

Surely, the German model is the way forward for football? The atmosphere would improve overnight, and ticket prices could be reduced – it costs as little as eight euros to stand on the Südtribüne in Dortmund. Football would once again be an affordable activity for the families that have been priced out of the game. Even the marketing men would be happy, as stadiums would be throbbing with the atmosphere so desperately craved by television producers and sponsors.

So, come on. The fans want it. Football needs it. Let's have a return to standing at football. And let's make it safe, to properly honour those fans that lost their lives watching the game they loved.

Saint & Greavsie

Saturday was the day that you made telly choices between strikingly similar fare:

BBC	v	ITV
Swapshop	v	*Tiswas*
Grandstand	v	*World of Sport*
Football Focus	v	*On the Ball*

On the Ball and *Football Focus* weren't really programmes. More a series of unrelated football features held together by their own linkman, who at the end of it all passed back to Des or Dickie. Presenters were one-dimensional, unable to show their feelings or personality. There was not much scope given for an ad-lib or a humorous aside.

Step forward, two of the greatest strikers of the modern era: one Englishman, one Scot. The English one played in the 1966 World Cup finals, turned out for a London club, and scored hat-tricks for fun. The Scottish one played in red, won countless trophies, and was idolised on the terraces. Welcome Geoff Hurst and Denis Law … err, hang on?

Ian St John and Jimmy Greaves roared on to our screens in the mid-1980s dressed in smoking jackets and cardigans. Both were cult heroes. Ian St John scored the winner in the 1965 Cup Final and was at the centre of countless Kop chants. Greaves scored goals wherever he went, but is best remembered for being dropped, albeit after injury, from the 1966 World Cup winning side. St John tried and failed at football management. Greaves battled the booze. How on earth could this work?

St John played the straight-laced lead as Greaves held court on everything from Scottish goalkeepers to women in football. The Scot often descended into fits of riotous laughter, drawing breath only to observe, "You slay me, Greavsie," while Greavsie repeated his mantra – as any thirty-something football fan will tell you, "It's a funny old game, Saint."

This harmless repartee paved the way for a host of presenter double acts. Where would Richard & Judy, Ant & Dec or Baddiel & Skinner be without these trailblazers?

There were also annuals. We should know: we've got two of them. Quite where *Football is Still a Funny Old Game* stands in the history of football literature, we can only guess.

Sky arrived and the television landscape changed forever. *Saint & Greavsie* were pulled. And, like *Metal Mickey*, they never returned. Not even on cable or satellite.

Scoring at both ends

No, not that sort of 'scoring at both ends'. Get your mind out of the gutter. Who do you think you are a professional footballer? We're talking own goals, the dark art of putting the ball through your own net.

Own goals are a fact of life. Play the game long enough and the law of averages dictates that a shot will shank off your knee, wrong foot the keeper, and condemn you to a life of ridicule – just ask Garry Mabbutt.

These days there seems no particular shame in scoring an own goal. Instead the culprit will shrug his shoulders, re-adjust his hair and get on with the arduous task of picking up forty-five grand a week. Own goal? Bothered.

There was a time, not so long ago, when a player would feel duty-bound to repay his debt to both teammates and fans. An own goal would have a profound effect on the perpetrator: he would play the rest of the game like a man possessed. Usually a defender, he would abandon his regular duties and embark on a kamikaze mission to score at the right end. And it usually worked. In fact, we seem to remember it happening every week. You couldn't switch on the radio on a Saturday afternoon without Stuart Hall or Jimmy Armfield mentioning how so-and-so had redeemed himself by scoring at both ends.

There was something almost biblical about it – the chance for instant atonement. Whatever it was, if a player scored an own goal, he would be hell bent on rectifying the situation.

Of course, the memory can play tricks on you. We were onvinced that Tommy Hutchinson's diving header in the 1981 FA Cup final was a spectacular response to his earlier own goal. It wasn't. The diving header came first, followed by a cruel deflection from a Glenn Hoddle free-kick.

But as a rule, scoring an own goal presented a unique opportunity to go from zero to hero over the course of ninety minutes. Shame today's players can't be arsed.

Scrapbook challenge

Is the humble scrapbook another victim of the 24-hour, multi-media age?

In our youth, everyone kept a scrapbook. WH Smith's had an entire section devoted to them. If your parents were flush with cash it was even possible to send away for a scrapbook in your favourite team's colours.

Every Sunday evening, you'd dutifully cut out the appropriate match report from the back of the paper. If you were really lucky there might even be a photo of some irrelevant midfield tussle (they never seemed to catch a goal or an incident of note on camera). You'd then glue the cutting into your scrapbook, writing the scores and date neatly alongside.

These scrapbooks were a labour of love. They were also important historical documents. What are today's kids going to show their grandchildren when asked about football in their day? A link to a defunct website doesn't have quite the same resonance.

Scrapbooks were great. They gave the appearance of being mildly educational, which meant you could delay doing your homework by protesting that you were updating your cuttings library.

Sadly, there's no place for them today. The back pages are now dominated by wildly inaccurate transfer speculation, while the sheer volume of column inches devoted to football would force you to start a new book every couple of weeks.

It is a real shame that scrapbooks are no more. We sincerely hope the government is bracing itself for a shortage of archivists and librarians about ten years from now.

Sex scandals

Dogging. Roasting. Mobile phones. Football has suffered from its fair share of sexual improprieties – but none of them compare to the scandal that rocked football during the summer of 1983.

For many of us it was the first time we'd encountered such behaviour, our first inkling that the nuclear family could be on the brink of meltdown. We refer, of course, to the trial separation of Roy Race from his wife, Penny.

Roy of the Rovers readers were still reeling from their hero's transfer from Melchester to Walford Rovers, when they were dealt another body blow – Penny and the kids had left Roy and jetted off to Crete. Racey had lost his beloved Melchester and was now on the verge of losing his family. To understand the magnitude of the situation, you have to understand that Roy was a surrogate father to many of us. After all, who wouldn't want a dad that managed a football club and was always available for a prolonged kickabout in the garden?

Things got worse as the summer continued. Roy was caught on camera escorting a mystery blonde to the Walford Supporters' Club dance. She turned out to be his personal assistant, the rather attractive Sandie Lewis. Roy and Sandie were never caught in flagrante but indiscretion was certainly implied. This was earth-shattering stuff. Surely, squeaky-clean Roy wouldn't indulge in something as clichéd as bonking his secretary? Would he?

The sorry affair dragged on until November when Roy's name was cleared and he was reunited with both Rovers and Penny. Racey was back with his family, and in true comic book fashion he scored a last-gasp winner in his first game back in Melchester colours. Normal service was resumed, but something was lost that summer – our innocence. Puberty beckoned, our hero was tarnished, and the world would never be the same again.

Shirt sponsors

Kisses. Hangovers. Shirt sponsors. Everyone remembers their first one.

For most thirty-somethings, that shirt sponsor would've been Hitachi. In the late 1970s, with Liverpool at the height of their domestic supremacy, school football practice was awash with kids in Liverpool shirts. It wasn't long before tops with 'Hitachi' emblazoned across their chests started appearing. As dim eight-year-olds, we didn't know what Hitachi made, but we didn't care because Kenny Dalglish wore one. We're sure that, to this day, there are plenty of people on the blue half of Merseyside who had absolutely no idea what a 'Hafnia' was either. We can picture the scene: "Just popping into town love." "Ohh, nip into Woolies and get us a bag of those new Hafnias will you." We're not attacking Scousers' intelligence here – far from it – in those early days of shirt sponsorship no one had a clue what the brash new lettering on football shirts was all about.

Liverpool and Hitachi were the most memorable pioneers of shirt sponsorship, but the first club to iron a sponsor's name onto their shirts were Kettering Town. In a Southern League match against Bath Town on 24th January 1976, Kettering quietly ushered in the sponsorship age. The Poppies ran out with the legend 'Kettering Tyres' on their shirts. The club soon found themselves in hot water with the FA, who ordered Kettering to remove the slogan. Manager, Derek Dougan, cleverly sidestepped the issue by altering the wording to read 'Kettering T', which – handily – also stood for Kettering Town.

The FA were reluctant, but the dam had burst. Before long clubs up and down the country were attracting shirt sponsors. The first few years of shirt sponsorship were gloriously innocent with the rules changing like the wind. For several years, clubs weren't allowed to appear on television sporting a sponsor's logo. Then there was a period when logos were restricted to a certain size for games on the telly. All this confusion led to some comedy moments, with teams who had brought the wrong shirts playing televised games with gaffer tape stuck over their sponsor's name.

Today, when even the arse of your average Football League player is sponsored, what benefit does this sponsorship actually bring? Do companies gain any kudos from an association with a middle-of-the-table side? Are fans really loyal to their sponsors? Nick was only eleven at the time, but he never seriously considered buying an Iveco truck as a result of their sponsorship deal with Watford.

In reality, the sponsors' logo is just there to ruin the look of the shirt. You might just about get away with a Carlsberg or a Vodafone, but pity the poor Brighton fans who had to walk round with 'NOBO' written large on their chests. And did Portsmouth supporters really buy replica shirts with that funny little heart logo plonked in the middle?

Even Barcelona have sold out. For years the distinctive red and blue striped shirt remained sponsor-free. But the start of the 2006/07 season saw Barca agree a deal with UNICEF to allow the charity's logo to be worn on the shirt for free. In addition the club agreed to donate a minimum of 1.5 million Euros a year to UNICEF. An admirable decision, although there's a nagging voice in our heads that thinks it could be the back door to full-scale sponsorship in the future.

Sponsorship ain't going away but there is a simple answer to those of us who deplore the tacky, mis-matched logos. Don't buy the shirt. Help is at hand: there are plenty of companies producing 100% cotton, sponsor-free, old-skool shirts, that are a damn sight better quality than all this newfangled polyester. Although, and we're not entirely sure this is a good thing, you can even buy retro-shirts with 'Hitachi' and 'Kettering Tyres' on the front. Nothing like reliving that first kiss, eh?

Simply dead

When Mick Hucknall announced that Simply Red were finished, an entire generation of footballers wept into their hot tubs. Footballers of a certain age loved Simply Red. How do we know? Because they listed them as their favourite band every bloody week in *Shoot!* magazine.

Simply Red. Not really a band, just Mick Hucknall and a bunch of other blokes. Go on, name us another member of Simply Red? See, we told you. And don't even mention the music. Yet footballers loved them. Even the great Roy Race put them down as his favourite band. And he was an effing cartoon character.

The only band to run them close were Dire Straits. Another group based around the talent of one man (names of the other three band members, anyone?). It was a simple case of middle of the road rock versus middle of the road pop? A real battle of the blands.

Anyway, what could footballers possibly like about a fast-car driving, crazy-haired millionaire who was always seen out with a gorgeous woman on his arm? Really, we can't see the connection. Oh yeah, who does Huckster support? Manchester United. QED.

Simply Red are dead. Long live Savage Garden.

Sky Sports News

For those of us too principled or just too tight to pay for a dish, Sky Sports News gives a sneaky peek at how the other half live.

Like the thousands of East Berliners who ran the gauntlet of the Stasi by picking up TV signals from the West, Sky Sports News grants us a glimpse of the unimaginable riches that lie beyond the humble Freeview box.

We can't help thinking that Sky have missed a trick here. After all, didn't the West German government beam over a cheery mix of pop videos and soap operas to show its communist neighbours what they were missing? Given this great opportunity to convert the masses, surely Sky could come up with something a little more enticing than Jeff Stelling and a bunch of ex-pros sitting in a studio relaying the action from a bank of television screens. Televisions screens that – for contractual reasons – we are not allowed to see?

The saving grace for Sky Sports News is the relentless stream of information and statistics that bombards you from every conceivable part of the screen. Where else can you simultaneously find out that David Nugent is out for a month with a suspected hernia and that AS Roma have been knocked out of the Italian League Cup? Oh, and that Georgie is a bit of a honey, isn't she?

Occasionally you even see some football. Albeit, from matches so unimportant that they have yet to be tied up in exclusive TV rights deals. But, hey, goals from Underhill, as Barnet take on Rochdale in the Autoglass Van Leyland Windscreen Cup, are better than no goals at all. For this reason alone, we remain loyal devotees to the information overload that is Sky Sports News. Well, that, and the fact we're too stingy to pay for the proper footy.

Snoccer

Flicking through old copies of *Roy of the Rovers* we stumbled across a half-page advert for Snoccer. For the uninitiated, Snoccer was the bastard child of snooker and, well, soccer. Only they didn't advertise it quite like that.

Rather optimistically, Snoccer was advertised as "The great new game of the '80s!" And to think, all these years, we'd assumed that rampant privatisation and the mass sale of council housing had been the 'great' game of the 1980s?

Snoccer, from the rather sketchy advert, appeared to consist of hitting velvet-bottomed players around the table hoping to deflect a snooker ball into the net. The craftsman-built mahogany tables were even available in two sizes, standard and deluxe, and you could get players in the colours of your favourite team. Or so the adverts claimed.

But even with snooker at the height of its popularity (during the 1980s, the entire population of the UK would tune in to watch colourful characters like Dennis Taylor and Willie Thorne do battle over the baize) this unlikely hybrid of football and bar-billiards was never going to catch on.

Then along came Pac-man and table-top games were doomed forever.

Stanchion, the

How will history remember Sir Trevor Brooking? For his headed goal in the 1980 FA Cup final? His late entrance as a substitute against Spain in the 1982 World Cup finals? Looking at least forty years old from the age of fifteen. Or for not looking a day over forty ever since? Perhaps, even for his short-lived 'Brooking's Briefs' slot on *Match of the Day* in the 1990s?

No, football fans of a certain age will remember him for *that* goal against Hungary in Budapest. The one when the ball got stuck in the stanchion. Impossible, younger readers cry – but no – it really happened. Sir Isaac Newton turned in his grave that night, as Sir Trev achieved the impossible – and in such an important match.

Luckily, in 1981, kids were free to try and recreate this scientific improbability throughout England's green and pleasant land. The goalpost police had not yet sprung into action, and every park or playing field had a set of goalposts with stanchions. That year, groups of boys spent hours trying to jam a football in the stanchion – just like Trev. Somewhere in East Anglia – where it is forever 1981 – there is still a stanchion with a ball wedged firmly in place.

Sadly, we will never see this feat repeated at a professional ground. Almost as amazing as Sir Trevor's perfect stanchion shot, was the sudden discovery that goalposts did not actually need stanchions to remain upright. The scientific formula is much too long to print here, but we can assure you that goalposts without stanchions are perfectly safe. Just not as much fun.

Storm boy

Myths and legends from the past, and rumours about the future, are an essential part of football's lifeblood.

We desperately cling to the great stories of yore, especially those that have become embellished and exaggerated with time. In contrast, rumours of exotic future signings give us hope for the future.

Here's a bit of first person narrative from Shaun's childhood, where myth and rumour collided head-on:

My story concerns Michael Laudrup. Laudrup was coveted by all of Europe's big clubs in the early 1980s, including Liverpool. I scoured the papers on a daily basis hoping for news of the signing. Foreign players were rare in England at the time, so to be linked with such a hot young talent was unusual. Media coverage in England was patchy at the best of times, and no footage of Laudrup was to be found on TV.

Then I read that, according to Danish legend, if you were born in a storm, you were destined for greatness – and, apparently, Michael Laudrup was born in a storm. That was it, Liverpool simply had to sign him. What a story… if he came to Liverpool he was bound to be great.

I'd imagined Laudrup's birth was accompanied by howling wind, torrents of rain, and almighty flashes of lightning – exactly the sort of storm that Michael Fish would've told you not to fret over. I'd imagined the family log cabin (I was only twelve: what could I do except believe outdated national stereotypes?) being attacked relentlessly by the elements, and the new baby's screams disappearing in the cacophony of noise.

Then he went and signed for Juventus. The fantasy was over. Bugger.

Maybe he wouldn't be that great anyway? Five La Liga titles in a row (four with Barcelona and the final one with Real Madrid); European Cup; Super Cup; Serie A title; Eredivisie title; twice Danish Player of the Year; twice Spanish Player of the Year; 104

caps for his country; voted Denmark's best-ever player in 2006; voted Spain's best foreign player 1974–1999; and knighted in Denmark. Nope, not that effing great. Thankfully Liverpool bought David Hodgson.

Ironically, Laudrup missed out on Denmark's greatest triumph. Like Cruyff and Schuster before him, Laudrup declined to play for his national team for a period. His brother Brian starred as Denmark won the European Championship in 1992. Even being born in a storm doesn't make you immune from the occasional error of judgement.

I recently heard that Steve McClaren was born in heavy fog and drizzle. I wonder what that means?

Strictly Celebrity Come Dancing on Ice

Can someone stop ex-footballers appearing on these damn TV shows? It's just plain embarrassing.

We understand that this sort of programme offers former weather girls, disgraced *Blue Peter* presenters and ageing glamour models another shot at celebrity, but the line between humiliation and redemption is perilously thin, and football players always end up looking stupid.

This humiliation is compounded by the fact that the show is usually won by a cricketer or a rugby player. This just confirms to the nation, what we knew already – footballers spent their entire childhood playing football, at the expense of everything else. If they left school with a CSE in woodwork they were a f**king genius. In contrast, not only did your average cricket or rugby star get a full set of A-levels and a place at Oxbridge, but they had time to take classes in ballroom dancing or learn how to ice skate. Clever bastards.

The line has to be drawn before someone gets hurt. It is only a matter of time before Andrew Lloyd Webber lures Martin Keown into a pair of roller skates to audition for *Celebrity Starlight Express*.

Stud pressure

Take a stroll down Hackney Marshes on a Sunday morning in September and you'll find scores of sweaty blokes hobbling around moaning about stud pressure.

Fear not, you've not stumbled into some low-budget porn production. These aren't well-hung lotharios complaining about the rigours of sustaining an erection with a camera crew looking on. No, they are Sunday footballers attempting to get through the first 90 minutes of the new season in brand new boots.

It is the unwritten law of Sunday football that the first game of each season takes place in gruelling 90-degree heat. This is punishment for a close-season spent sitting in front of the telly eating pizza. It also ensures that you have to run around in new boots on a surface that closely resembles concrete. The stud pressure is enormous, and the blisters – quite frankly – are horrific.

Stupid o'clock kick-offs

Things used to be so simple. Five days a week you'd get up, early doors, and go to school, or at least pretend to. Saturdays would be a quick trip to the shops, home for lunch, then off to the football. If you couldn't get to the game, you'd sit through the wrestling on *World of Sport* waiting for the right moment to switch over to the vidiprinter on *Grandstand* (see Grandstand's vidiprinter and the space-time continuum). On the seventh day you would rest.

This schedule was set in stone. Games would kick off at 3.00pm on a Saturday, with midweek matches being played on a Tuesday or Wednesday at 7.30pm or 7.45pm. There were one or two notable exceptions: Tranmere Rovers favoured Friday night games, reasoning they would pick up floating fans from Liverpool and Everton; Stockport County employed a similar tactic, wise to the plethora of options available to football fans in the Greater Manchester area; and Torquay United, under the stewardship of Frank O'Farrell, clocked up impressive attendances by playing on a Saturday night. But that was pretty much it.

Fast-forward thirty years, and you've not got an effing clue when your team is supposed to be playing. Every June the new season's fixtures are published, and, for a couple of glorious days, you look forward to nine months of Saturday afternoon football with a few midweek games thrown in for good measure. Then the bastard television companies get involved.

One week, you are kicking off at 4.10pm on a Sunday, the next week it's 12.45pm or 5.15pm on the Saturday; following that you could be assigned the dreaded 8.00pm Monday night graveyard slot.

If you're really unlucky, you get to factor in European competition, which sprawls uncontrollably across the middle of the week. It's a total nightmare. You can't plan anything because, if you do, the bloody fixture will get moved – just so it can be beamed live to hundreds of deserted pubs around the UK.

This sorry affair reached a nadir on the weekend of 6/7th October 2007, when, out of the ten Premier League matches scheduled, only Aston Villa versus West Ham United kicked off at 3.00pm on a Saturday. To us, this is an utter disgrace. Yes, life moves on and working patterns change – we no longer all pour out of the factory and into the football ground on a Saturday afternoon, in scenes reminiscent of Lowry's *The Match* – but there is something to be said for tradition. It's not right to expect loyal fans to juggle work, family and social commitments in order to attend a game of football, especially one at the other end of the country, scheduled for 8.00pm on a Monday night.

Football is more than a hobby – it's a religion. And, as such, we need to know when and where to worship.

Trouble is, it's only us that's bothered. On the same weekend that Villa and West Ham took part in the only top-flight game to kick-off at 3.00pm on a Saturday, *Football Focus* revealed the results of a survey of more than 1,000 fans. When asked if they objected to football fixtures being moved from the traditional Saturday 3.00pm kick-off, 62 per cent replied "no". It would seem stupid o'clock kick-offs are here to stay, as now we have a whole generation of fans who have grown up with matches kicking off at any time of night and day.

In another twenty years, 3.00pm kick-offs will be a distant memory, and football will never be the same again.

Sweet and tender hooligans

We're the first to admit that we spend most of our waking hours wandering round in a nostalgia-induced daze, wishing it was 1982. And not just because we were three stone lighter and not greying at the temples, but because football was so much better then. There is, however, one aspect of 'old' football that can't be viewed through our rose-tinted spectacles – hooliganism.

Make no mistake, things were pretty bad at the end of the 1970s and beginning of the '80s. Everyone remembers Scotland fans ransacking Wembley in 1977 or Millwall fans ripping up seats and hurling them at the police at Kenilworth Road in 1985, but the hooligan problem ran much deeper. Almost every law-abiding fan that travelled to matches in the 1970s or '80s will recall getting caught up in trouble at some stage.

As an eleven-year-old boy, Nick remembers a Boxing Day afternoon standing on the away terrace at Kenilworth Road, having missiles chucked at him by a handful of home 'fans'. A year later he was on a bus from the station to St Andrews for an FA Cup quarter-final when a group of youths appeared from a side street and lobbed a brick at the window (it bounced off). Nick and his Dad weren't hardcore ultras looking for a scrap; they were just there to enjoy the football. Watford, weren't exactly renowned for their hooligan element – so heaven knows what it was like supporting a more high-profile team.

Football hit rock bottom in the 1980s. The terrible loss of life at Heysel and English clubs' subsequent ban from European competition were unquestionable low points. But gradually, things changed. The reasons were complex and intertwined – the Taylor Report, increased ticket prices, Gazza's tears (see Tears of a clown), they all played a part. Now, twenty years on, it is even possible for England fans to travel to a World Cup without needing to completely trash the country they are visiting. Korea and Japan in 2002 was never going to be a hooligan-fest due, in part, to geography, but Germany 2006 could have been a nightmare. Instead, the hooligans stayed at home and were replaced by normal fans intent on having a good time.

So we don't lament the passing of football hooliganism, but what really pisses us off is the industry that has grown up around it. We understand there is a need to document the sociological phenomenon of hooliganism, but for every book like *Hooligan Wars – Causes and Effects of Football Violence*, edited by Mark Perryman, there's a mountain of self-congratulating dross glorifying hooligan activity.

It seems it is not enough to have a shameful past of beating rival fans to a pulp or smashing up town squares across Europe – you now have to write a bloody book about it. But hey, it's okay, we're all grown-up now. We've got kids and mortgages and have long since retired from a life of senseless violence.

The pulp fiction is bad enough, but the movies are worse. We've had Gary Oldman as the yuppie hooligan in *The Firm* and Danny Dyer in *The Football Factory* – both "gritty, realistic portrayals of the hooligan scene" or "grim and depressing excuses for wanton violence" depending on your perspective. The coup de grâce came in September 2005, with the release of the laughable *Green Street*. In a stroke of comedy genius, the Hobbit, aka Elijah Wood, was cast as a naive American who gets the bug for football violence. Casting Bilbo Baggins as a member of the ICF would've taken the biscuit had it not been for Charlie Hunnam's attempt at a cock-er-nee accent. It made Dick Van Dyke look like a pearly king. Make it stop. Hooliganism is not worth glorifying – in print or on screen.

The only crumb of comfort we can draw from this plethora of books and films is that the hooligans have decided to sit at home on their Burberry sofas with a nice cup of tea and a muffin. These days, the hoolies seem content with watching the violence on DVD. For this we should be grateful.

Tears of a clown

If it wasn't Nick Hornby's fault (see Nick Hornby), then it must have been Gazza's.

The Premier League, Champions League, stupid o'clock kick-offs, ridiculous wages, oligarchs, identikit stadia – you name it – they can all be traced back to Paul Gascoigne's actions at the 1990 World Cup.

Italia '90 was, without doubt, one of the dullest World Cups on record. Cameroon aside, the football was dour and the only excitement came in the form of endless penalty shoot-outs. Yet the tournament is fondly remembered, and often cited as the turning-point in modern football. Why? Because Gazza cried. Like a girl.

In the ninth minute of extra time, with the scores level at 1-1, Gascoigne caught Thomas Berthold with a lunging tackle and was shown a yellow card – a yellow card that would, had England triumphed over West Germany, have cost Gascoigne his place in the World Cup final. The booking was a fair call by the referee, but harsh on Gazza, who had played like a man possessed. All game Gascoigne had the look of a kid living out a childhood fantasy. Equally, his reaction to the booking was that of a child on Christmas Eve being told that Santa Claus didn't exist.

Gazza had been living the dream for all of us – nineteen years old, playing in a World Cup semi-final – so when that dream turned into a nightmare, can anyone really blame him for blubbing? It was a moment of such fragility that it touched an entire nation.

Before we knew it, Gazza was being held up as an example of that ghastly 1990s media creation the 'new man'. Why? Because he was a bloke. And he wasn't afraid to cry. In public. Of course, Gazza, in his own inimitable style, undermined those 'new man' credentials just days later, pratting about on an open-top bus wearing comedy breasts.

In hindsight, we're not sure how much Gazza's tears contributed to the whole 'new man' phenomenon, but they certainly changed football – forever. Suddenly, you could talk about football, at school or around the watercooler in the office, without being written off as a social deviant.

He might have been as daft as a brush, but Gascoigne had achieved something that for years seemed totally unobtainable... he'd made football cool again.

The September after the 1990 World Cup, college freshers were amazed to find that, along with the giant iconic images of Bob Marley or The Clash, you could also buy a four-foot poster of Gazza sobbing into his shirt (ideal for papering over the mould in a student bedsit). All of a sudden, Gazza was a student icon, giving Che Guevara a run for his money in the UK's halls of residence.

Post-Italia '90, the crowds, slowly, started to return to the English game. Media interest mushroomed and the scene was set for some of the most drastic changes in the game's history. And all because a young, insanely talented Geordie kid burst into tears.

Ten thousand leagues under the Premiership

From the amount of media coverage it receives you'd assume the Premier League was the only league in England. It isn't.

More and more people are shunning the so-called 'best league in the world' and getting their football fix elsewhere.

It would probably come as a surprise to most top-flight chairmen, but there's a thriving non-league scene out there. From the Conference down to Step Seven of the non-league game (the lowest official step of the national non-league pyramid), there are over eighty divisions. Beyond that there are numerous feeder leagues. Add to that women's football, youth, reserve and Sunday leagues, and you've got a whole lot of football going on.

From the 'McGirls Money Management Bedfordshire Premier' to the 'Taulke Finance Worthing & District Division One' there are an awful lot of people dedicated to the game beyond the confines of the Premiership.

We urge you all to find your local club, get down there and give it a try. It sure as hell won't set you back £40 a ticket. Top-flight chairmen take note.

Think of a number

Remember when shirts were numbered 1 to 11, and not festooned with players' names and sponsorship logos? Happy days.

Numbers used to mean something back then. Fighting your way through the scrum to look at the school noticeboard, you knew instantly that if you were listed as number three on the team sheet you were consigned to another game at left-back. How you envied anyone handed the number nine shirt and, thus, a game at centre-forward.

Numbering shirts from 1 to 11 had been introduced in the late 1920s and, despite opposition from traditionalists, was formally adopted in 1939. The numbering followed the 2-3-5 formation favoured at the time, with numbers two and three being full-backs, three to six half-backs and seven to eleven forwards. This eventually evolved into the more commonly used 4-4-2 formation, although when we were at junior school in the mid-1970s, 2-3-5 was still all the rage with the school caretaker who doubled up as our football coach.

In the days before managers started playing mind-games with each other, the 1 to 11 system was great: as soon as the team sheet was handed in or read out over the tannoy, coaches and fans alike knew how a team was going to line up. Nowadays, it is a numerical free-for-all.

It was the introduction of squad numbers that really screwed things up. Squad numbers used to be the exclusive domain of the international tournament and, as such, they seemed exotic and extravagant – exactly the sort of fancy continental touch that would be frowned upon in the hurly-burly of the football league.

We loved the quirks that squad numbers threw up at the World Cup. The Dutch got the ball rolling in 1974, assigning shirt numbers in alphabetical order for everyone except Johan Cruyff, who insisted on wearing the number 14. This was nothing, Cruyff also wore a special shirt with just two stripes running down the sleeve; due to a contract with Puma, he couldn't be seen to endorse a rival manufacturer's kit.

In both the 1978 and 1982 World Cups Argentina employed a similar system. Thus, in 1982, we were treated to the sight of Ossie Ardiles running around in midfield wearing the number one shirt (he was pipped to the post in '78 by Noberto Alonso of River Plate). England tried it in 1982, although they excluded goalkeepers and Kevin Keegan from the equation. The keepers wore one, 13 and 22, whilst King Kev got to wear the number seven shirt. The rest of the squad were numbered alphabetically, from Viv Anderson at number two down to Tony Woodcock at 21. But squad numbers were just for World Cups. They would never catch on at league level, surely?

Then, at the start of the 1993/94 season, it happened. The Premier League adopted squad numbers, also adding players' names to the back of shirts. Once again, traditionalists baulked.

In the next few years, professional leagues around the world followed suit. And it wasn't too long before pretentious Sunday League sides also started using squad numbers.

We wonder if any top-flight club has fielded a team numbered 1 to 11 since the introduction of squad numbers. We wonder, but we can't be arsed to look.

Now the curios that used to be the exclusive domain of the World Cup occur on a weekly basis. In fact, it has all got a bit silly.

When Iván Zamorano joined Inter Milan, he found Ronaldo occupying his number nine shirt, so quick as a flash, he decided to wear the number 18 shirt, but cleverly inserted a '+' between the one and the eight to make nine. Genius. Becks could've done something similar, when Raul refused to budge from the number seven shirt at Real Madrid. Instead, David opted for the number 23 shirt, favoured by American basketball legend Michael Jordan. This was a brilliant bit of foresight by Team Beckham that endeared him to American audiences years before his transfer to a Galaxy far, far away.

Since their introduction, squad numbers have been creeping higher and higher. In 2003, Vítor Baía, the FC Porto goalkeeper, wore the number 99 in the European Cup final. Cristiano Lucarelli (see Left-wingers) wore the number 99 shirt for both AS Livorno and Shakhtar Donetsk, in honour of Livorno's left-wing ultras group Brigate Autonome Livornesi (although since his return to Italy with Parma he has dropped a digit, wearing number nine instead).

After the death of his mother, Adolfo 'Bofo' Bautista wore a shirt with 100 on the back for Mexican side, Club Deportivo Guadalajara. He also opted to have the name his mother called him, 'Bofo My Angel', printed on the back of his shirt (he is even referred to in this way in the computer game *FIFA07*). Since his transfer to Jaguares de Chiapas, he has worn the number one shirt.

For obvious reasons, Moroccan international, Hicham 'Zero' Zerouali wore a zero on his shirt for Aberdeen (tragically, he died in a car accident in Rabat in December 2004).

Then in the 2007 Merseyside derby, Steven Gerrard and James Beattie wore shirts with '08' on them, to promote Liverpool's status as European City of Culture in 2008.

These examples are just the tip of the iceberg. Squad numbers on shirts have changed everything. You can no longer glance down at your programme and assume the bloke wearing the number three shirt is a left-back or the number nine a lumbering centre-forward. These days it has all gone a bit 'Johnny Ball'. Go on, "Think of a number." Someone will be wearing it.

This goalie's got guts

A crisis in English goalkeeping? Too right there is.

At Mexico '70, when Gordon Banks was struck down with a bout of Montezuma's Revenge, did the nation panic? Of course it didn't. We had an able deputy in Peter Bonetti. 'The Cat' simply stood in for Banksy as we eased past West Germany and went on to win another glorious World Cup. Oh, hang on. Sorry, our mistake.

In the 1970s our keepers were the envy of the world. We had so many we didn't know what to do with them. Even Ron Greenwood gave up. He couldn't decide who was better, Ray Clemence or Peter Shilton and so, in the greatest example of appeasement since Neville Chamberlain, he would let Ray play one game and Shilts the next. Pity poor old Joe Corrigan: he was arguably just as good as the other two, but rarely got a game.

The wheels started coming off in the 1990s when the England management let some bloke go in goal sporting a ponytail. Up until then, goalkeeping had been the last bastion of the 'real man'. Hard as nails, a keeper wouldn't think twice about diving headlong into a ruck of players, emerging several blows to the head later, with the ball. And that was in training. They also had hands like shovels and arms at least three feet long (a result of a childhood spent hanging from door frames).

According to stereotype, goalkeepers were also a little bit mental. The sort of zany guys who would have taped the classic 1970s office witticism, "You don't have to be mad to work here, but it helps" to the crossbar, if the rules allowed it.

Referees afforded keepers no favours. The thinking was: if you were stupid enough to want to play in goal, you probably enjoyed the danger. From the playground to the top division, if the keeper was on the floor clasping the ball it was a striker's divine right to try and kick it out of his hands. No one complained, and no one ever awarded a free-kick. These days, if anyone so much as looks in the general direction of a goalkeeper, the ref is blowing on his whistle like a man possessed. As a result, keepers have evolved into timid little creatures, scared of crowds and loud noises.

Anyway, back to ponytails. We can't imagine Peter Shilton with a ponytail – a bubble-perm yes, but not a ponytail.

Things have got so bad that we long for England's keepers to pick up a mystery stomach bug. Not just one keeper – all of them. We'd probably stand a better chance of keeping a clean sheet if we stuck Crouchy in nets.

Goalies used to have guts. Not any more.

Tight fit

Everything that goes around comes around. One day, even the 1970s 'footballer's beard' will be back in fashion. We can't bloody wait... The Mickey Droy revival? Bring it on.

However, there's one football fashion that will never return: the tight-fitting shorts worn by players in the early to mid-1980s. We challenge you to look back at a photograph from the era and not wince.

Forget Joan Collins in *The Stud*. In the '80s, there was more over-stretched nylon on show at your local league ground. It wasn't just risqué. It was downright dangerous. We're surprised any of those guys managed to have children. No wonder Vinnie Jones squeezed Gazza's nuts... they were right there, bursting out of a cheap nylon prison.

Didn't those shorts hurt? How did players run at full pelt, let alone attempt a change of direction? Put some of today's superstars in a pair of 1980s shorts and they'd be next to useless.

We've seen old-fashioned cotton football shirts sell by the thousand, even the early '80s pin-stripe shirt has made a surprise comeback, but aside from the football-crazed fetishist, there'll never be enough demand to facilitate a tight-fitting shorts revival. Thank heavens for that.

Tim Vickery – Voice of a generation

The Beat Generation had Ginsberg, Burroughs and Kerouac. Generation X (the closest thing we had to a genuine literary yoof movement) had Douglas Coupland. Today's young hipsters have JK Rowling.

Football's not all that different. First came Charles Buchan, with his imaginatively titled *Charles Buchan's Football Monthly*. Then there was Brian Glanville, who has been writing about the beautiful game for longer than anyone cares to remember. But now, there is a new pretender to the throne. His name is Tim Vickery.

In an age when football is covered-to-death in the media, it is all the more surprising that one man should rise to the top. Listeners to BBC Radio Five Live's *World Football Phone-In* will know him as the 'Legendinho'. We've no idea how tall he is, but on the radio he certainly comes across as a little legend.

The *World Football Phone-In*, presented by the excellent Dotun Adebayo, has something of a cult following. The show is on air every Saturday morning at around 2.30am, although people without a sleeping disorder can download it as a podcast. It differs from the myriad of football phone-ins by actively shunning the domestic game. This is world football, and the Premiership only gets a look-in when they discuss potential signings from around the globe. Actually, it's more hardcore than that: phone with a question about European football when Dortun's got his South American or African correspondents on the show and you'll get short shrift (in the nicest possible way).

This is where Tim Vickery comes in. He is the BBC's South American football correspondent. He's based in Rio de Janeiro, and he frequently fights for airspace with his dog, who makes an audible appearance most weeks. Barking dogs aside, there is nothing Tim doesn't know about South American football. Callers will inquire about a left-back who has made three appearances for Botafago and Tim will know all about him. The man is amazing. We can only aspire to this depth of knowledge.

Tim also contributes a regular column on South American football to the BBC's website. He even made his silver screen debut, as a radio announcer, in *The Game of Their Lives*, a film about the United States' famous appearance at the 1950 World Cup in Brazil (yep, the one where they beat an England side containing Tom Finney, Billy Wright and Alf Ramsey).

Tim Vickery is the voice of a generation. He is the number one choice for fans who care to look beyond the Premier League. We can't help thinking he is destined for even greater things. We just hope he's still in Rio come 2014, because we quite fancy crashing at his flat, even if all that barking stops us getting much sleep.

Totò Schillaci

Is Totò Schillaci the only man in history to have "blessed the rains down in Africa" and been the top scorer at a World Cup? Yep, "as sure as Kilimanjaro rises like Olympus above the Serengeti", he was (see Rock Me Amadeus for an explanation, of sorts).

Trophy presentations

Modern-day trophy presentations are crap.

Back in the 1970s, every kid in the land knew exactly how many steps they'd have to climb to lift the FA Cup: thirty-nine.

Generations of players, riddled with cramp (another Cup Final staple), hauled themselves up the famous Wembley steps to collect their medals from Princess Michael of Kent (it was always Princess Michael, wasn't it?). Protocol insisted that the captain went first. He wiped his palms on his shirt, shook a few hands, kissed the cup, and lifted it above his head to an almighty roar from the victorious fans. Each player then took his turn at kissing and lifting the cup, to steadily diminishing cheers. Sometimes, the manager followed sheepishly at the back. Players would then be showered with scarves and stupid hats as they descended from the Royal Box, spilling onto the pitch for a lap of honour. This protocol was hardly ever broken, but when it was it was for the grandest of gestures. After Oxford United defeated QPR in the 1986 Milk Cup final, manager Maurice Smith gave up his winner's medal and allowed long-serving club trainer Ken Fish to climb the thirty-nine steps.

Wembley was the most famous example, but almost every stadium hosting a big final used the same tried and tested formula. Up some steps, lift the trophy, down some steps. Simple.

These days, picking up a trophy is a branding exercise. At the final whistle a team of technicians rush onto the pitch to assemble a shaky-looking platform adorned with sponsors' logos. The players hang around for eternity as the stage is bolted together. Then, after the losing team, the match officials, ballboys and assorted dignitaries have shuffled gloomily across the makeshift stage, the winners get to collect their trophy. Even this takes forever, as the whole squad troop across to collect their medals. Finally, with the stage visibly groaning under the weight of twenty-two blokes bouncing around in a state of delirium, the winning captain gets to lift the bloody trophy. We've no idea what happens next, as the podium is either engulfed in a cloud of smoke, generated by half a ton of fireworks, or the players are buried under a mountain of glitter. Then, just as the clouds begin to part, the television coverage cuts to the bloody adverts.

The suits in charge of designing the new Wembley Stadium obviously shared our concerns. Trophy presentations at Wembley have reverted to the Royal Box. It's an admirable nod to tradition. Unfortunately, instead of thirty-nine steps, the players have to climb 107 to collect the trophy. The ascent is so laborious that they disappear from view for a good few minutes, no doubt stopping to refuel on prawn sandwiches. Perhaps they should've invested in a lift? Or that travelator thing they used on *Gladiators*?

TV goths

Oh no, it's all gone Emo.

Are Alan Hansen and Gabby Logan involved in a secret competition to see who can wear the most eyeliner?

Now Gab has joined the Beeb, do we have a full-scale goth revival on our hands? Was that *Welcome to the Black Parade* by My Chemical Romance accompanying Goal of the Month? Stop it, before someone gets hurt.

Ugly rumours

The element of surprise has completely disappeared. The advent of 24-hour sports news on the telly, phone-ins, and the internet has resulted in fans knowing which club a player has signed for before the ink has dried on his contract.

In the old days, a transfer might not even make the back page of the paper. If you didn't regularly scour the sports section, you could easily miss a whole swathe of transfer activity. You could turn up to the first game of the season not realising half the team had been sold during the summer recess. No one phoned you, sent you unsolicited emails or splashed news of a transfer on the front cover of *Roy of the Rovers*. Things just happened. Occasionally, a major transfer would be mentioned at the end of *John Craven's Newsround*, but only if they couldn't run a funny story about pandas.

Back then, it was as if the transfer fairy decreed – overnight – that the player should move clubs. There were no protracted wrangles over money, dramatic U-turns or desperate 'come and get me pleas'.

On completion of a transfer, there would be a shot of the player in his new club's shirt. Failing that, holding a scarf aloft alongside his new manager was the preferred option. What followed was a collection of quotes that could be found in the PFA transfer handbook:

"It was an easy decision to make"
"I spoke to the manager and I could tell he wanted me"
"This club has great potential"
"They play the style of football I like"
"This club is a sleeping giant "

That was it. Done deal. Brown paper bags binned.

There then followed a period of integration. A game for the reserves, a place on the bench, and finally, a full debut. Then, for the next eighteen months, John Motson would chuckle, and remind you of the transfer tag hanging heavily around the player's neck.

You were shocked and astounded, of course. Shaun thinks that a friend broke the news about Ian Rush's transfer back to Liverpool from Juventus on a minibus en route to Port Isaac for a brass band concert. He didn't believe it. No one had told him before it happened. No one at school had checked their mobile for the latest news.

Beckham to LA Galaxy? Apparently the *Daily Mail* announced it as far back as October 2006. It wasn't announced, it was a bloody logical guess. If you guess enough, eventually you'll guess right. In the old days, it didn't seem right to guess about footballers' careers, less so to brag about being right. Funnily enough, we have never seen a back page headline admitting they got it wrong.

We're sure there were transfer talks and contractual meetings in the past, but we didn't need to know every detail. These days agents, clubs, families, friends and teammates all leak stories to the press. The rumour mill is an industry in its own right. Rumours sell papers, so much so that when the transfer actually goes through, the newsmen are long gone. They've lost interest and moved on to the next sensational – probably not true – transfer scoop.

Wankdorf Stadium

We can't quite believe it. But it is on Wikipedia, so it must be true. Yep, they've only gone and knocked down the great Wankdorf stadium. Without telling us.

For years, the Swiss side, Young Boys Bern and the Wankdorf stadium were improbable bedfellows. It was common knowledge across the playgrounds of Britain, and never failed to raise a smutty laugh. We sat through years and years of *A Question of Sport*, hoping-against-hope that David Coleman would ask the name of Young Boys Bern's home ground. We longed to scream "WANKDORF" at the telly, and we waited in vain to see how Bill Beaumont and Beefy Botham would react. It never happened, and it probably never will.

The Wankdorf did, however, earn its place in football folklore for something other than its dubious name. It hosted the 1954 World Cup Final, dubbed the 'Miracle of Bern', when West Germany earned a remarkable victory over Puskás' legendary Hungarian side. Germany came back from being 2-0 down after just eight minutes to win 3-2, in a game that had enormous ramifications for both countries. For West Germany the victory began the process of healing for a nation still suffering the consequences of the Second World War. For Hungary the defeat is often cited as a contributing factor to the Hungarian Revolution of 1956, when the people rose up against the Soviet-backed government. Puskás and many members of the Mighty Magyars were playing for Honvéd in a European Cup tie in Bilbao at the time of the uprising. Many of them, Puskás' included, never returned, opting instead for a career with clubs in Western Europe.

So next time someone mentions the Wankdorf Stadium, try not to laugh. It's really not funny.

Wankie FC

Wankie FC – three times winners of Zimbabwe's Castle Cup (1970, 1973 and 1991). No, it's really not funny.

Waterlogged pitches

Football is an outdoor game. It rains outdoors. A game should not be called off unless there is serious risk of injury to players. How many top-flight players have died drowning? Muddy pitches and a bit of rain make for a far better spectacle.

Games are called off for waterlogged pitches all too readily. Fair enough, on the odd occasion, a pitch might just be too wet. Forgive us for being simple, but how hard is it to design something to cover the pitch if heavy rain is imminent? Perhaps something plastic that could be rolled out quickly, working in tandem with a gutter around the pitch to drain the water away? How f**king hard is that? It seems to work at Wimbledon. And guess what? It would stop snow getting on the pitch as well. Not that we're against snow. Far from it. In fact, we'd prefer it if all games in December and January were played on a snow-covered pitch. Adverse weather conditions? Bring 'em on.

What not to wear

Football is a simple game. What clothes to wear when playing it? Even simpler.

Playing a match: football boots (on grass) or football trainers (on Astroturf or indoors), shin pads, football socks, football shorts, football shirt. End of.

But go to any indoor league in Britain and you will see a wide array of non-essential football attire being worn.

A favourite accoutrement of the young 'fashionable' player is the slip-on trainer. They might as well be wearing slippers. Yet still they persevere. Our first thought is, "You tosser – one, equally fashionable, broken metatarsal coming right up." How many times does the trainer come off in the tackle? Yep, every single time. Combine the slip-on trainer with white ankle socks, and you've got our favourite type of opponent – a player who is not prepared for any physical contact. The game is as good as won.

Tracksuit bottoms or jogging pants are not football attire either, especially indoors. Okay, a goalie can get away with it, as they are throwing themselves around on hard surfaces. But how can you take anyone seriously who runs around indoors in a tracksuit? It is not cold. And, if it's protection they want, wearing trackie bottoms is not the way to stop you being kicked. It's like a red rag to a bull for anyone in our age group. Tracksuit-clad legs are just begging to be kicked. Your PE teacher always wore a tracksuit indoors, and what did you long to do to him?

Wearing tracksuit bottoms is a pretty horrific offence, but playing in a pair of those stupid three-quarter-length bottoms – the ones that stop abruptly, halfway down your calf – is a crime against humanity. Why don't these idiots just be done with it and tattoo "I AM A COCK" on their foreheads?

Add all this to a sleeveless T-shirt and you have a person not playing football as we know it. They are kicking a ball, but not playing football.

Football's attire is both its strength and its weakness. True, it is a simple game that can be played anywhere while wearing pretty much anything, but there has to be a limit.

Next time you see someone in the street wearing slip-on trainers, give them a kick from us.

Wideboys

According to our battered old *Rothmans Football Yearbook* from the early 1990s, Oldham Athletic's Boundary Park pitch measures a respectable 106 x 72 yards. Nowadays, for internationals and Champions League matches, FIFA and UEFA have stipulated that all pitches should measure 105 x 68 (metric) metres. This uniformity is all well and good but, as kids, pitch boundaries during park kickabouts were never so clearly defined.

'Jumpers for goalposts' (see Jumpers for goalposts) was the easy part. Sure, the goals could be made bigger or smaller at the behest of a bored goalkeeper, but otherwise the piles of jumpers, bags and coats fairly accurately defined either end of the pitch. Setting width boundaries was another matter entirely.

Down the rec, no one wanted to be messing about with throw-ins. After all, what was the point? There was no referee, let alone linesmen. If there were no natural, physical or geo-graphical boundaries – rivers, hedges, main roads – the width of the pitch was determined by how far players were prepared to travel in pursuit of the ball. This wasn't a problem for the majority of the game, as most of the play would be confined to the centre of the pitch. However, once or twice a match, the boundary of the pitch would be tested to its absolute limit.

It always happened like this:

Two kids would give chase to a long, misdirected kick from the keeper. One kid would get to the ball first and attempt to beat his opponent. Only, instead of cutting inside and heading for goal, the tussle would head in the opposite direction. The two combatants would become dots on the horizon; sometimes they would disappear from view altogether. Protocol determined that no one else would be sent to fetch them. This was a personal dual, hombre-contra-hombre. They could be gone for hours. The rest of the kids would readily accept this break in proceedings and lounge about in the goalmouth talking about the previous night's telly or getting out the Panini cards to go through the whole "Got. Got. Swap" routine (see Figurine Panini).

When the two players finally returned – one running full pelt with the ball, the other jogging, less enthusiastically behind – no questions were asked; everyone else just jumped up and got on with the game. If one of the players came back sopping wet, he'd just shrug his shoulders and get on with it. Coming back with the ball was a matter of honour, and if that meant wading through a murky stream, so be it.

We can't help thinking that football's ruling elite could learn a thing or two from these impromptu games. Rather than the endless pursuit of conformity and a homogeneous pitch size, perhaps they should live a little and embrace pitches without boundaries. The thought of Ashley Cole and Cristiano Ronaldo disappearing down the tunnel after a loose ball – never to be seen again – gives us a lovely warm feeling inside. Go on, Sepp, give it a whirl…

Without further Adu...

By the time you read this Jozy Altidore will be the new Freddy Adu.

You see, Jozy is the latest MLS teen sensation to catch the eye of European talent scouts (see Championing the wonderkids). And much like Freddy Adu, Jozy has that Peter Pan quality about him: he is destined (in the eyes of the media at least) to remain seventeen forever.

Altidore blazed a trail from an early age. He has represented the US at Under-17, Under-20 and full international level. According to his website he "had three multi-goal games" in the 2005 World Championships (no, we're not quite sure what that means either, but you've got to admit it sounds impressive). He also scored his first goal for the US senior side in a friendly against Mexico in February 2008.

Jozy was also the youngest player to score a goal in an MLS play-off game, when he grabbed New York Red Bull's only goal in a 2-1 defeat at the hands of DC United in 2006. He's even appeared on the cover of the American version of *FIFA 08*, standing shoulder to shoulder with Ronaldinho. The lad is clearly going places... let's hope the sheer weight of expectancy doesn't get the better of him.

World Cup Willie

"Er, love, fancy a bit of World Cup Willie?"

Tip and Tap, Pique the sombrero-wearing chilli pepper, and that cute little orange fellow from Espana '82 – there's been some truly great World Cup mascots over the years, but only one of them became a euphemism for sex.

It may have been the swinging sixties, but not everyone was dropping acid or appearing naked on a West End stage. The majority of English folk were still very reserved about sex. However, hosting the World Cup provided a rare opportunity for a bit of the other. Up and down the country, as England's matches came to an end, the man of the house would switch off the television, turn to his missus and say, "Love, how about a bit of World Cup Willie?"

Take a quick look at the England and Wales population census and you'll see a sharp spike in the birth rate about nine months after that memorable 4-2 win over West Germany. Probably.

Year zero

The 1992/93 season is football's very own 'year zero'.

From the way some commentators and pundits go on, you'd think the game had been invented over a nice cold glass of Chablis, in the summer of 1992. Highly unlikely, as that summer the UK was under siege from the twin perils of new-age travellers and dangerous dogs. At some point during the July, it got really serious as the two evils converged when the new-agers armed themselves with big scary dogs. War on terror? Pah. Try facing-off a stoned hippy toting a pretty angry Springer Spaniel.

Anyway, we digress, back to Year Zero. This might be something of a wake-up call to fans of the armchair and the remote control, but the Football League had been doing a grand old job for the previous 100-odd years – a fact anyone who attended the Mercantile Credit Centenary match between a Football League Representative side and a Rest of the World XI in August 1987 will testify. What a game! What a day out!

But everyone buys into this myth. Fans will tell you that Manchester United have won the title ten times, Arsenal three, Chelsea two, Blackburn Rovers once and, of course, Liverpool never. This is simply not true.

Don't you see? All they did was change the name and sex it up a bit. The Premier League, for all the hype, is still just the latest brand name for English football's top tier. The proper trophy tally for the teams listed above reads: Liverpool eighteen titles, Manchester United seventeen, Arsenal thirteen, Blackburn Rovers and Chelsea three apiece. This puts a slightly different spin on things. Although we feel it our duty to remind Liverpool supporters that they've not won a title since 1989/90.

In our darkest hours, we begrudgingly accept that there is no going back and that the Premiership has become one of the most successful leagues in the world. But, please, please, please – stop rewriting football history.

Yo-yo clubs

When we were kids yo-yos were an after-school activity – not a football phenomenon.

Such is the disparity between the top flight and the Championship, that some clubs openly aspire to yo-yo status. To us, that's aspiring to be deeply average. Sure, it is almost impossible to bridge the financial gulf that exists between the two leagues, but where's the spirit? The grasping of the nettle, the chance to give the big boys a bloody nose? And, if you really can't compete, then a season in the top flight should be treated as a great opportunity to go down fighting by kicking those highly-paid fancy-dans up-in-the-air, at every available opportunity.

Other clubs don't actually want to yo-yo, it is just a fate that befalls them. The West Midlands must be the yo-yo capital of England, as Birmingham, West Brom and Wolves have all bounced back and forth between the top two divisions in recent years.

Perhaps it's not the clubs' fault. Gone are the days when Nottingham Forest won promotion from the Second Division and followed it the very next season by winning the First Division title (upping the ante even further by winning the European Cup two years in a row in 1979 and 1980). Money has sullied ambition. In a world where you are rewarded to the tune of £30 million for finishing bottom of the league, retaining your top-flight status is a bonus. Big business pulls the strings, and yo-yo clubs are here to stay.

"You're listening to Five Live from the BBC"

We love Five Live, but there's one thing about the station that really gets our goat: the commentators insist on inserting the phrase "You're listening to Five Live from the BBC" into a match commentary at every available opportunity.

Guess what? We worked out we were listening to Five Live when we tuned in our bloody radio. Our nice new DAB digital radio even displays the station name on a primitive LCD display.

What do they think we do when we switch on the wireless? Randomly spin the dial and see where we land? Hmmm, not such a bad idea.

Zinedine Zidane

Pinochet. Pol Pot. Stalin. In the days that followed the 2006 World Cup final these guys had nothing on Zinedine Zidane. He was the devil incarnate. Zidane's crime? Nutting an Italian centre-half. Big wow.

The world's media couldn't understand how a man of Zidane's brilliance could carry out such a crude act of violence. But was it really that bad? If Zizou had really intended to hurt Materazzi, surely he would've nutted him on the forehead, not tamely butted him in the chest.

Why the moral outcry? Sure, it was the World Cup final and Zizou's last ever match – but what an exit! As early as the sixth minute, when Zidane chipped his penalty in off the bar, it seemed he was walking the tightrope between genius and madness. Contrary to popular opinion the headbutt actually enhanced his iconic status. After all, he's not the first genius to have a bit of a wayward streak. He's just the next in a long line of slightly unhinged football legends more than happy to hit the self-destruct button. Think Maradona. Think Cantona. Whisper it, even the great Pelé was prone to the occasional sending-off.

Anyway, the media seemed to conveniently forget that Zidane was no angel. He was sent off a total of fourteen times during his career including a dismissal, for a crude stamp on Saudi Arabia's Fuad, en route to winning the 1998 World Cup.

Come on everyone, loosen up. Let the headbutt go. Our only regret is that instead of trudging forlornly past the World Cup trophy on the way back to the dressing room, he didn't knock the bloody thing off its rostrum. Now that would've been a proper tantrum.

By way of a postscript, only FIFA could issue a player who has just retired from competitive football with a three-match ban. Inspired.